W9-CCC-778

Kids·Kids·Kids

40
winning designs
from the
Knitter's Magazine contest

 BOOKS

Contributors

Melissa Adams

Barbara Albright

Suzanne Atkinson

Leslie Ann Bestor

Cindy Brook

Kaye Durnin Canfield

Lorraine Ehrlinger

Margaret Fisher

Kerry Fletcher-Garbisch

Susannah Heath

Mary Lee Herrick

Rowena Hill

Claire Kellogg

Jill Kent

Rita Garrity Knudson

Erin Kosich

Cindy Kuo

Lana Lowenkamp

Katherine Matthews

Hester Meyers

Anndora Morginson

Leslie Munro

Valerie Prideaux

Margaret K.K. Radcliffe

Jill Ramos

Camille Remme

Martha H. Rickey

Jaime Shafer

Irene Sinclair

Katharina Smietana

Ann B. Strong

Kelly Ward

Leonore Z. Wells

Kate Winkler

Andrea A. Wong

Joyce Renee Wyatt

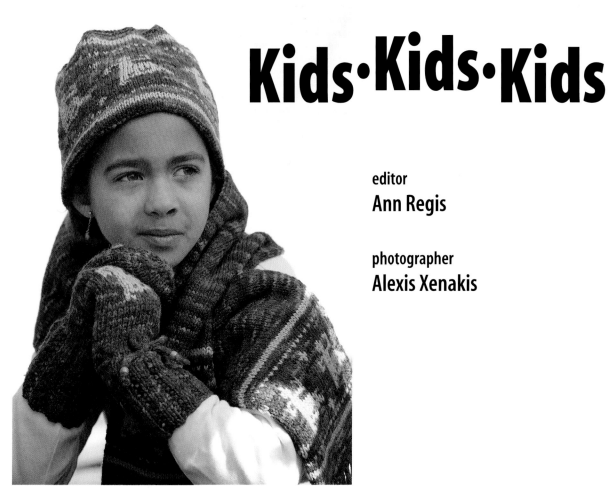

Kids·Kids·Kids

editor
Ann Regis

photographer
Alexis Xenakis

Credits

AN XRX BOOK

PUBLISHER
Alexis Yiorgos Xenakis
EDITOR
Ann Regis
INSTRUCTION EDITING
Traci Bunkers
Gitta Schrade
FASHION DIRECTOR
Nancy J. Thomas
PHOTOGRAPHER
Alexis Yiorgos Xenakis
PUBLISHING DIRECTOR
David Xenakis
GRAPHIC DESIGNER
Bob Natz
BOOK PRODUCTION MANAGER
Lynda Selle
DIGITAL COLOR SPECIALIST
Daren Morgan
PRODUCTION ARTISTS
Debbie Gage
Kellie Meissner
Jay Reeve
Carol Skallerud
MARKETING DIRECTOR
Tad Anderson

FIRST PUBLISHED IN USA IN 1999 BY XRX, INC.
PO BOX 1525, SIOUX FALLS, SD 57101-1525

COPYRIGHT © 1999 XRX, INC.

All rights reserved.
No part of this publication may be reproduced, stored in a retrieval system,
or transmitted, in any form or by any means, electronic, mechanical,
photocopying, recording or otherwise, without the prior permission
of the copyright holder.

We give permission to readers to photocopy the instructions and graphics
for personal use only.

ISBN 0-9646391-7-3

Produced in Sioux Falls, South Dakota, by XRX, Inc., 605.338.2450

Printed in Hong Kong

In this book, we've highlighted 40 projects from the 94 entries in the Knitter's Magazine Kids Contest. Many wonderful knitters sent us so many wonderful knits. And the sharing didn't stop there. Here's what they had to say:

Inspiration...

I've designed a tunic-style sweater to fit my lovely, dumpling-shaped niece Lydia. Katherine Matthews, Lydia's Lace, p. 16

I make this little sweater and bonnet for my children and nieces and nephews as a link to their great-grandmother. Hester Meyers, With Love, p. 18

Levin and I had seen a puppet show, so St George and the Dragon became his 4th-birthday sweater. Kerry Fletcher-Garbisch, St George and the Dragon, p. 34

I started knitting for my first grandchild Celia.... Anndora Morginson, A Twist of Lime, p. 38

This sweater was inspired by the beautiful ethnic household textiles of Guatemala.... Martha H. Rickey, Panuelo #2, p. 54

It amazes me that a small garment could represent so much in my life. Cindy Brook, Beribboned!, p. 56

The inspiration...came after taking a class...with designer Debbie Bliss.... Erin Kosich, Hey, Frosty!, p. 82

I designed this coat for my granddaughter, using yarn inherited from my mother. Lorraine Ehrlinger, Ana's Lopi Coat, p. 80

Kids are full of light and energy and this should be reflected in the bright clothes they wear. Cindy Kuo, Candy Cane, p. 61

I knit for my two daughters...my daughter Amaran...my granddaughter Alaina...my friend's 5-yr-old Natalie...my daughter Carolie...my niece Willow's new baby Kiana...my daughter Jerina....

Participation...

My granddaughter Courtney started me knitting when she wanted doll clothes. Katharina Smietana, Pink People!, p. 71

Over the years at my children's requests, I have made brown and gold striped tigers, sharks, bumblebees.... Lenore Z. Wells, Puppets Galore!, p. 72

My granddaughter was seven when she helped me dye the yarn and knit the sweater. Irene Sinclair, Emily's Sweater, p. 32

When knitting for our daughter Bethany, I involve her in the selection of colors.... Suzanne Atkinson, A Matched Set, p. 76

What yarn do I use when knitting for children? Any yarn I like—as long as it's soft. Lana Lowenkamp, Hairy One, p. 19

My best advice for knitting toys for children is to make them very tiny or go really big.... Suzannah Heath, The Pony, p. 96

Recognition...

Thanks to all the knitters who have reminded us how fun, fanciful and personal knitting can be. Thanks to the children who inspired them (and then let us keep their knits for as long as we needed). Here's to happy knitting and happy kids!

Foreword

Oh dear, what can the matter be?

Oh, dear, what can the matter be?

Dear, dear, what can the matter be?

Oh, dear, what can the matter be?

Johnny's so long at the fair.

He promised to buy me a bunch of blue ribbons;

He promised to buy me some bonny blue ribbons;

He promised to buy me a bunch of blue ribbons,

To bind up my bonny brown hair.

Contents

BEFORE YOU BEGIN . . .

Kids' sweaters are so much fun to knit! Even if a complicated design is involved, the small size makes it a quick knit. And the delighted faces of the recipients make it all worth while. Here are a some suggestions for following our patterns.

Level

Although we've indicated a skill level for each pattern, use that as a guide, not a deterrent! In general, beginner patterns will write out techniques and procedures while intermediate or experienced patterns are more streamlined. Scan through a pattern and make note of unusual techniques or construction methods. Sometimes, simple clarification is all you may need to tackle a more advanced project.

Abbreviations and terms

Knitting instructions seem like shorthand to many people. A quick review of the abbreviations on the next page will refresh your memory .

Sizes

Directions are written for the smallest size with larger sizes in parentheses. If there is only one number or set of instructions, it applies to all sizes.
Our patterns are sized from measurements compiled from a variety of sources including the National Bureau of Standards and the ready-to-wear and home sewing industries. Use the finished measurements rather than the age of the child as a guide in choosing what size to make. Some 2-year-olds can be hefty!

Gauge and Needles

These are the key ingredients to any successful project. Do take the time to knit a small swatch with the yarn you intend to use. For example, if the gauge is 20 stitches to 4"/10cm in stockinette stitch using size 8 (5mm) needles, cast on 20 stitches and work at least 2" in stockinette stitch. If your piece is narrower than 4", change to larger needles. If it is wider, change to smaller needles. Don't try to knit looser or tighter—let the needles do the work! It does not matter what size needles you use as long as you get the gauge called for in the pattern. Your gauge may change slightly when you knit the actual piece. Measure your work at regular intervals to make sure you are on track!

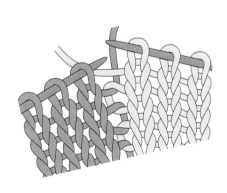

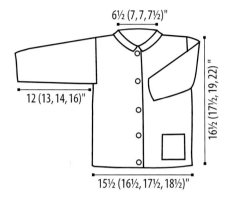

6½ (7, 7, 7½)"

12 (13, 14, 16)"

16½ (17½, 19, 22)"

15½ (16½, 17½, 18½)"

Flag

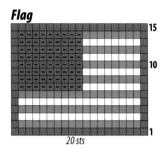

15

10

1

20 sts

USA

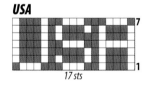

7

1

17 sts

Chart 1

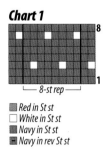

8

1

8-st rep

■ Red in St st
□ White in St st
■ Navy in St st
■ Navy in rev St st

Year

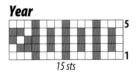

15 sts

Yarns

We have given generic yarn information for each project because many of the yarns that were used are no longer available. Use our yarn guide (see below) to help identify the proper yarn weights.

It is always a good idea to purchase a little more yarn than called for in the pattern. You can always make a small item such as a hat or finger puppet with any left-over yarn. Your local knit shop can also guide you as to yarn quantities for specific brands.

If you already have yarn and don't have yardage information per ball, weigh your yarn and see how it compares with the total weight called for in the pattern. For example, a garment may require 6 balls of sport weight yarn, each 1¾oz, or a total of 10½oz. Your pile of sport weight yarn should weigh at least 10 or 10½oz to ensure successful completion of that project.

Techniques

You may not be familiar with a specific knitting or finishing technique called for in a pattern. For example, some people always use 3-needle bind-off to join their shoulder seams. Others have never heard of this technique. Our advice is two-fold. First and foremost, use the technique you feel most comfortable with—knitting should be a pleasure, not a pain! Having said that, why not try a new technique. Acquiring new skills can streamline the knitting process and stretch your creativity. Easy does it. Practice the technique on scrap yarn to make sure you are doing it properly. Once you've got the hang of it, go back to your project and do it for real! Use pages 10–13 to refresh your memory.

Metrics

To convert inches to centimeters, multiply the inches by 2.5.
For example: 4" x 2.5 = 10cm

To convert feet to centimeters, multiply the feet by 30.48.
For example: 2' x 30.48 = 60.96cm

To convert yards to meters, multiply the yards by .9144.
For example: 4 yds x .9144 = 3.66m

Abbreviations

approx approximate(ly)
beg begin(ning)(s)
CC contrasting color
cn cable needle
cm centimeter(s)
cont continu(e)(ed)(es)(ing)
dc double crochet
dec decrease(e)(ed)(es)(ing)
dpn double-pointed needle(s)
foll follow(s)(ing)
g gram(s)
" inch(es)
' foot(feet)
inc increas(e)(ed)(es)(ing)
k knit(ting)(s)(ted)
lb pound(s)
m meter(s)
mm millimeter(s)
MC main color
oz ounce(s)
p purl(ed)(ing)(s)
pat(s) pattern(s)
pm place marker
psso pass slipped stitch(es) over
rem remain(s)(ing)
rep repeat(s)
rev reverse(d)
RS right side(s)
rnd round(s)
sl slip(ped)(ping)
ssk slip, slip, knit 2tog
st(s) stitch(es)
St st stockinette stitch
tog together
WS wrong side(s)
wyib with yarn in back
wyif with yarn in front
yd(s) yard(s)
yo yarn over

Yarn Weights

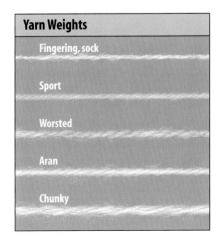

Fingering, sock

Sport

Worsted

Aran

Chunky

Chain st

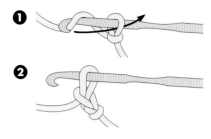

Slip st crochet

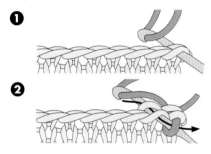

Single crochet

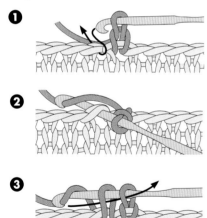

Crochet for knitters:

Chain st (ch)

1 Make slip knot, yarn over hook, draw yarn through loop on hook.
2 First chain made.

Slip st crochet (sl st)

1 Insert the crochet hook into the fabric, catch the yarn, and pull up a loop.
2 Go into the next stitch of the fabric and draw a new loop through the fabric and the loop on the hook, leaving one loop on the hook. Make each loop a little loose so the edge won't be tight. Repeat this step to the end.

Single crochet (sc)

Work slip stitch to begin.
1 Insert hook into next stitch.
2 Yarn over and through stitch; 2 loops on hook.
3 Yarn over and through both loops on hook; single crochet completed. Repeat Steps 1-3.

Reverse single crochet (rev sc)

1 Reverse direction of work; work from left to right. **1a** Work a slip stitch to begin. **1b** Enter hook into next stitch to right.
2 Bring yarn through stitch only. As soon as hook clears the stitch, flip your wrist (and the hook). **2a** There are now two loops on the hook, and the loop just made is to the front of the hook (left of the old loop).
3 Yarn over and through both loops on hook; reverse single crochet completed.
4 Continue working to right, repeating from Step 1b.

Double crochet (dc)

1 Yarn over, insert hook into next stitch. Yarn over and through stitch only. There are now 3 loops on the hook.
2 Yarn over and through 2 loops on hook.
3 Yarn over and through remaining 2 loops on hook.

Reverse single crochet

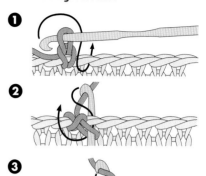

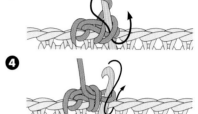

Double crochet

Intarsia

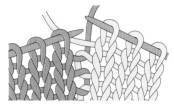

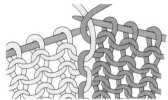

Intarsia

When changing from one color to the next when working intarsia, it is necessary to twist the yarns to prevent holes. Pick up the new color from under the old color, as shown, and continue working.

Yarnover (yo) Depending on the context, yarnovers are made differently.

K, yo, k After knitting a stitch, the yarn is behind the right needle. Bring the yarn under the needle to the front, take it over the needle to the back (where it is in position to knit), and knit the next stitch.

K, yo, p Knit, bring yarn under the needle to the front, over the needle to the back, then back under the needle to the front before you purl the next stitch.

P, yo, k Purl, the yarn is already to the front of the needle so simply bring it back over the needle; it is in position to knit the next stitch.

P, yo, p Purl, bring yarn over the needle to the back, then bring it under the needle to the front before you purl the next stitch.

Lifted increase For a right increase, knit into right loop of next st in the row below (1), knit into next st (2). For a left increase, knit into left loop of last st knitted in the row below (3).

Short row wrap

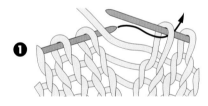

Uses Each short row adds two rows of knitting across a section of the work. Since the work is turned before completing a row, stitches must be wrapped at the turn to prevent holes.

1 To wrap a stitch: with yarn in back, slip next stitch as if to purl. Bring yarn to front of work and slip stitch back to left needle as shown. Turn work.

2 When you come to the wrap on a right-side row, make it less visible by working the wrap together with the stitch it wraps.

Mattress stitch

Mattress stitch seams are quite invisible. They require selvage stitches (which are taken into the seam allowance) and are worked with right side facing.

1 After blocking, thread blunt needle with matching yarn.

2 Working between selvage stitch and next stitch (in diagram, selvage stitch is darker), pick up 2 bars.

3 Cross to matching place in opposite piece, and pick up 2 bars.

4 Return to first piece, go down into the hole you came out of, and pick up 2 bars.

5 Return to opposite piece, go down into the hole you came out of, and pick up 2 bars.

6 Repeat steps 4 and 5 across, pulling thread taut as you go.

Mattress stitch

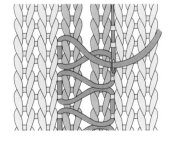

Yarnovers

K, yo, k

K, yo, p

P, yo, k

P, yo, p

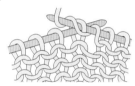

Lifted increase

Make 1

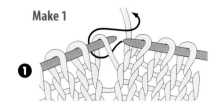

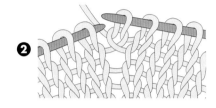

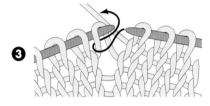

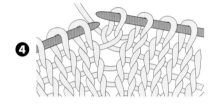

Ssk

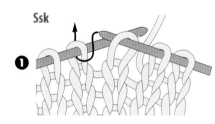

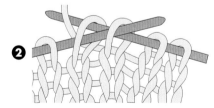

Duplicate stitch

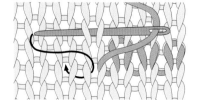

Make 1 (Single increase, M1.)

1. With right needle from back of work, pick up strand between last st knitted and next st. Place on left needle and knit through back (or purl through back for M1 purlwise).

2. This increase can be used as the left increase in a paired increase (M1L).

3. For the right paired increase, with left needle from back of work, pick up strand between last stitch knitted and next stitch. Knit twisted.

4. This is a right M1 (M1R).

Ssk *Uses* ssk is a left-slanting single decrease.

1 Slip 2 sts separately to right needle as if to knit.

2 Knit these 2 sts together by slipping left needle into them from left to right. 2 sts become one.

S2KP2, SSKP, sl2-k1-p2sso

Uses A centered double decrease.

1. Slip 2 sts together to right needle as if to knit.

2. Knit next st.

3. Pass 2 slipped sts over knit st and off right needle.

4. Completed: 3 sts become 1; the center st is on top.

S2PP2

Uses A centered double decrease worked on the purl side.

1 Slip 2 stitches separately to right needle as if to knit.

2 Slip these 2 stitches back onto left needle. Insert right needle through their 'back loops,' into the second stitch and then the first and slip 2 sts to right needle.

3 Purl next st.

4 Pass 2 slipped sts over purl st and off right needle. 3 sts become 1; the center st is on top.

Duplicate stitch

Duplicate stitch (also known as Swiss darning) is just that: with a blunt tapestry needle threaded with a length of yarn of a contrasting color, cover a knitted stitch with an embroidered stitch of the same shape.

Backward loop cast-on *Uses* To cast on a few stitches for a button-hole or the start of a sleeve.

Form required number of backward loops:

1 Loop the yarn over your left thumb. Insert the needle into the loop.

2 Slip loop off thumb and tighten: one stitch cast on.

S2KP2, SSKP, sl2-k1-p2sso

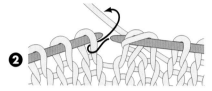

S2PP2

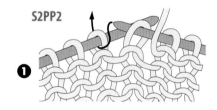

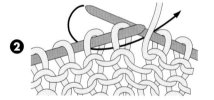

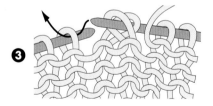

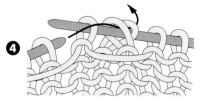

Backward loop cast-on

❶

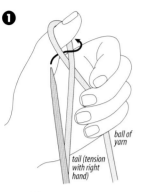

ball of yarn

tail (tension with right hand)

❷

Cable cast-on

❶

❷

❸

Chain cast-on

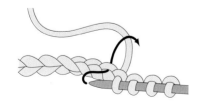

Cable cast-on

Uses A cast-on that is useful when adding stitches within the work.
1 Make a slipknot on left needle.
2 Working into this knot's loop, knit a stitch and place it on left needle.
3 Insert right needle between the last two stitches. From this position, knit a stitch and place it on left needle. Repeat step 3 for each additional stitch.

Chain cast-on *Uses* As a temporary cast-on.
Chain desired number with scrap yarn. With main yarn, knit up one stitch in each chain, inserting needle into back loops of crochet.

3-needle bind-off *Uses* Instead of binding off stitches and sewing.
Seam effect. Place right sides together, back stitches on one needle and front stitches on another. *K2tog (1 from front needle and 1 from back needle). Rep from* once. Bind first stitch off over 2nd stitch. Continue to k2tog (1 front stitch and 1 back stitch) and bind off across.
Ridge effect. Place wrong sides together, then work as above.

Bind off in pattern As you work the bind-off row, knit or purl the stitches as the pattern stitch requires. Try the same technique on cast-on rows.

Fringe
1 Fold six strands of yarn in half and draw the folded end through the edge of the knitted fabric using a crochet hook.
2 Draw the loose ends of yarn through the loop, and draw up firmly to form a knot. Trim ends.

Tassels
1 Wrap yarn around a piece of cardboard that is the desired length of the tassel. Thread a strand of yarn, insert it through the cardboard and tie it at the top, leaving a long end to wrap around the tassel.
2 Cut the lower edge to free the wrapped strands. Wrap the long end of the yarn around the upper edge and insert the yarn into the top, as shown. Trim the strands.

3-st I-cord I-cord is a tiny tube of stockinette stitch, made with 2 double-pointed needles.
1 Cast on 3 sts.
2 *Knit 3. Do not turn work. Slide stitches to right end of needle. Rep from *.

3-needle bind-off

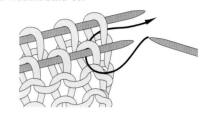

Fringe

❶   **❷**

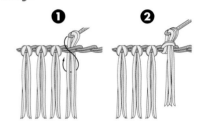

Tassels

❶   **❷**

3-st I-cord

hush·a·bye, baby...

KIDS CONTEST

Hush-a-bye, baby,

Way up on high,

Never mind, baby,

Mommy is nigh,

Swinging the baby

All around,

Hush-a-bye, baby,

Up hill and down.

Infants

Lydia's Lace

INTERMEDIATE

EDITOR'S NOTE   This garment is knit in one piece to the armhole, then divided into backs and front.

I've noticed that the sweaters that my baby niece Lydia wears tend to ride up over her tummy because of her diaper bulge and because she is lovely and dumpling-shaped! So, I've designed a tunic-style sweater which is slightly flared under the arms and which buttons up the back. My sister Kelly, Lydia's mom, says it will look perfect with tights or trousers and reminds me that young babies need flat buttons on the back.

I think this would also look nice as a pinafore. Instead of knitting sleeves, I'd just finish off with garter stitch around the armholes. If this were lengthened and the buttons extended down the back, it could be a knitted dress. I'm looking forward to trying out these variations and coming up with larger sizes as Lydia grows older.

Oriel lace pat (multiple of 12 sts plus 1)
Rows 1, 3, and 5 (RS) P1, *ssk, k3, yo, p1, yo, k3, k2tog, p1; rep from*.
Rows 2, 4, 6, and 8 K1, *p5, k1; rep from*.
Row 7 P1, *yo, k3, k2tog, p1, ssk, k3, yo, p1; rep from*.
Row 9 P2, *yo, k2, k2tog, p1, ssk, k2, yo, p3; rep from*, end last rep p2.
Row 10 K2, *p4, k1, p4, k3; rep from*, end last rep k2.
Row 11 P3, *yo, k1, k2tog, p1, ssk, k1, yo, p5; rep from*, end last rep p3.
Row 12 K3, *p3, k1, p3, k5; rep from*, end last rep k3.
Row 13 P4, *yo, k2tog, p1, ssk, yo, p7; rep from*, end last rep p4.
Row 14 K4, *p2, k1, p2, k7; rep from*, end last rep k4.
Rows 15, 17, and 19 Rep row 7.
Rows 16, 18, 20, and 22 Rep row 2.
Row 21 Rep row 1.
Row 23 P1, *ssk, k2, yo, p3, yo, k2, k2tog, p1; rep from*.
Row 24 K1, *p4, k3, p4, k1, rep from*.
Row 25 P1, *ssk, k1, yo, p5, yo, k1, k2tog, p1; rep from*.
Row 26 K1, *p3, k5, p3, k1; rep from*.
Row 27 P1, *ssk, yo, p7, yo, k2tog, p1; rep from*.
Row 28 K1, *p2, k7, p2, k1; rep from*.
Body
Cast on 157 sts. K 4 rows. Work rows 1-28 of Oriel lace pat, then rep rows 1-13 once. **Next (dec) row (WS) For size 3 months** K1, *k1, k2tog; rep from* across—105 sts. **For size 6 months** K1, *k2, k2tog; rep from* across—118 sts. **For size 9 months** K1, *k3, k2tog; rep from* across, end k1—126 sts.
For all sizes K 4 rows for garter st ridge. Beg with a k row, work 6 (8, 10) rows in St st.
Divide for backs and front
Next row (RS) K24 (27, 29) sts (left back), bind off next 4 sts (armhole), k until there are 49 (56, 60) sts on right-hand

Sizes 3 (6, 9) months. Shown in size 3 months.
Finished measurements Chest (buttoned) 18 (20, 22)". Length 11 (11½, 12)".
Yarns 3 (4, 4) balls sport weight yarn (each 1¾oz/50g, approx 136yd/125m) in Teal.
Needles One pair size 5 (3.75mm) needles, *or size to obtain gauge.*
Extras Stitch holders. Four ¼" flat buttons.
Gauge 24 sts and 32 rows to 4" (10cm) over St st using size 5 (3.75mm) needles.

BACK

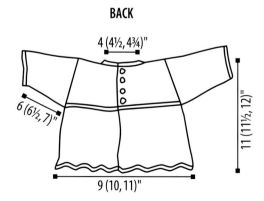

4 (4½, 4¾)"

6 (6½, 7)"

11 (11½, 12)"

9 (10, 11)"

needle for front, bind off next 4 sts (armhole), k to end (right back). Cut yarn and place first and last 24 (27, 29) sts on hold.

Front

With RS facing, join yarn and k 1 row, then p 1 row across 49 (56, 60) sts of front. K next row and dec 1 st each side—47 (54, 58) sts. Cont in St st until piece measures approx 2½" inches above garter ridge, end with a WS row.

Shape neck

Next row (RS) K17 (19, 20), place next 13 (16, 18) sts on hold, join a 2nd ball of yarn and k to end. Working both sides at same time, bind off 3 sts from each neck edge once. Dec 1 st at each neck edge every other row twice. Work even on rem 12 (14, 15) sts each side until piece measures 4 (4¼, 4½)" from garter ridge. Place all sts on hold.

Left Back

With RS facing, join yarn at center back and k 1 row, then p 1 row over 24 (27, 29) sts. K next row and dec 1 st at end of row. Work even on 23 (26, 28) sts until piece measures same as front to shoulder. Place sts on hold.

Right Back

With RS facing, join yarn at armhole and k 1 row, then p 1 row over 24 (27, 29) sts. K next row and dec 1 st at beg of row. Work even on 23 (26, 28) sts until piece measures same as front to shoulder. Place sts on hold.

Sleeves

Cast on 42 (44, 46) sts. K 4 rows. Cont in St st, AT SAME TIME, inc 1 st each side every 4th row 9 times—60 (62, 64) sts. Work even until piece measures 6 (6½, 7)" from beg, end with a WS row. Bind off 2 sts at beg of next 4 rows. Bind off rem sts.

Finishing

Block pieces, pinning out scalloped edge of lace pat. Using 3-needle bind-off, work shoulders tog, leaving 11 (12, 13) sts at each centerback on hold.

Neck

With RS facing, beg at left back neck edge and pick up and k evenly around neck, working all sts on hold at left and right back and at centerfront. K 4 rows. Bind off all sts loosely.

Buttonband

With RS facing, beg at lower edge of left back and pick up and k evenly to neck edge. K 6 rows. Bind off loosely. Place 4 markers for buttons, the first ½" below neck edge and 3 others spaced approx 1" apart.

Buttonhole band

With RS facing, beg at neck edge and pick up and k evenly along right back to lower edge. K 6 rows, working buttonholes as foll: On row 3, bind off 2 sts opposite each marker. On row 4, cast on 2 sts over each set of bound-off sts.

Set in sleeves. Sew sleeve seams. Sew buttons on.

This garment buttons up the back.
Use flat buttons for baby's comfort.

With Love

ADVANCED BEGINNER

When my grandmother died in 1959, I was given her knitting bag which had a sweater-in-progress in it. I finished that little sweater and have been making it and this bonnet ever since. I make them for my children and nieces and nephews as a link to their great-grandmother, Alta Taylor Sherman.

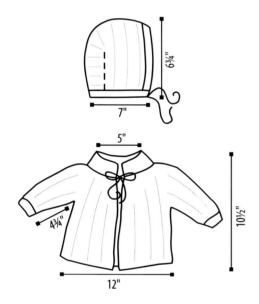

6¾"

7"

5"

4¾"

10½"

12"

Size 6 months.

Finished measurements Chest approx 24". Length 10½".

Yarns 5 balls in sport weight yarn (each 1¾oz/50g, approx 136yd/125m) in Variegated Pastels for sweater and bonnet.

Needles One pair size 4 (3.5mm) needles, or size to obtain gauge. Size 4 (3.5mm) double-pointed needles for I-cord.

Extras Stitch holders.

Gauge 24 sts and 48 rows to 4" (10cm) over garter st using size 4 (3.5mm) needles.

EDITOR'S NOTE This garment is worked from side to side in one piece. Keep careful track of rows!

Right Front

Cast on 63 stitches. K 2 rows. Work short rows as foll: **Row 1** (RS) K49, turn and leave rem 14 sts unworked (these 14 sts will form the collar). **Row 2** Sl first st purlwise, k48. Turn. **Rows 3-4** Rep rows 1-2. **Rows 5-6** K63. These last 6 rows formed 3 ridges. Rep last 6 rows 15 times more. There are 48 ridges from beg plus the first ridge from first 2 knit rows.

Shape right sleeve

Row 1 K63. Turn. **Row 2** K35 and place rem 28 sts on hold. Cast on 28 sts (sleeve) and turn—63 sts. **Row 3** K49, turn and leave rem 14 sts unworked (collar). **Row 4** Sl first st purlwise, k41, leave rem 7 sts unworked (sleeve cuff). Turn. **Row 5** Sl first st purlwise, k55, turn. **Row 6** K63. The last 4 rows formed 2 ridges. Rep rows 3-6 a total of 20 times more—42 ridges from sleeve cast-on. **Next row** Bind off 28 sts, k to end. **Next row** K35, then pick up and k 28 sts of body on hold—63 sts. Mark this row.

Shape back

Rep rows 1-6 of right front 24 times—there are 72 ridges at lower edge of back from marked row.

Shape left sleeve

Work as for right sleeve.

Shape left front

Rep rows 1-6 of right front 16 times—48 ridges. K 2 rows, binding off on 2nd row.

Finishing

Block piece lightly. Sew sleeve seams. Work a 3-st I-cord 30" long, to fit around neck. Weave through lower edge of collar and tie into bow. If desired, work 1 row single crochet evenly around entire jacket.

BONNET

Cast on 76 sts. Work 7 rows in k2, p2 rib.

Beg pat: **Row 1** Knit. **Row 2** Purl. **Row 3** Knit. Rep last 3 rows 17 times more—9 'purl' stripes. **Next row** Bind off 26 sts, k to end—50 sts. Rep last row once more—24 sts. Make 9 more 'purl' stripes by working pat rows 1-3 a total of 18 times. Place sts on hold. Sew sides of narrow section to bound-off sts of wide section. With RS facing, beg at ribbing and pick up and k27 sts along side edge of wide section; work [k2, k2tog] 6 times across 24 sts on hold; rep from*; pick up and k27 sts along other sid/e section—72 sts. Work ½" in St st. Work 7 rows in k2, p2 rib. Bind off in rib. Make two 3-st I-cord straps, each 13" long. Sew to sides of bonnet.

Bonnet assembly

Center back (neck edge)

Narrow section

Wide section

Front

ADVANCED BEGINNER

EDITOR'S NOTE   This garment is knit in one piece to the armhole, then joined with the sleeves into a circularly knit yoke. Do not cut yarns at end of rows; carry them loosely up the side of work.

Body

With A, cast on 133 (145, 153) sts. K 4 rows. *Change to 1 strand each B and C held tog. **Beg rev St st: Row 1** (RS) Knit. **Row 2** Knit. **Row 3** Purl. **Row 4** Knit. Change to A. Rep rows 1-4. Rep from* until piece measures 6 (6½, 7)" from beg, end with a RS row 3. **Next row** (WS) K34 (37, 39), bind off next 4 sts (underarm), k until there are 57 (63, 67) sts on right needle, bind off next 4 sts (underarm), k to end. Place all sts on hold.

Sleeves

With A, cast on 49 (53, 55) sts. K 4 rows. Change to 1 strand each B and C held tog and work 4-row stripe pat as for body until piece measures 3½ (4, 5)" from beg, end with same RS row 3 as for body. **Next row** (WS) Bind off 2 sts, k to last 2 sts, bind off last 2 sts. Cut yarn, fasten off last st. Place all other sts on hold.

Join body and sleeves

With RS facing and ready to work row 1 of stripe pat across body, k34 (37, 39) (right front), place marker, k45 (49, 51) sts of one sleeve, place marker, k57 (63, 67) sts of back, place marker, k across 2nd sleeve, place marker, k across 34 (37, 39) sts of left front—215 (235, 247) sts. **Beg raglan shaping** Work rows 2-4 of stripe pat and dec 1 st before and after each marker on row 3—8 sts dec'd. Cont to dec 1 st each side of markers every RS row 16 (18, 20) times more, AT SAME TIME, work first buttonhole on next RS row (k4, yo, k2tog), then work 2 more buttonholes approx 1½" apart—19 (22, 24) sts rem on each front, end with a WS row. **Shape neck** Cont raglan shaping, bind off 5 (6, 6) sts at beg of next 2 rows. Dec 1 st at each neck edge every RS row 4 times—8 sts on each front, 23 (25, 25) sts across back. Dec each side of sleeve until 7 sts rem across each sleeve. Bind off all sts loosely.

Finishing

Block piece very lightly. With RS facing and A, join yarn and work 1 row sc evenly around neck. Sew underarm and sleeve seams. Sew buttons on.

What yarn do I use when knitting
for children? Any yarn I like—
as long as it is soft!
I love going to yarn shops,
finding goodies in the end of lot basket
and holding them for the right time.
In this case, I didn't have enough
for a grown-up
but plenty for a baby jacket

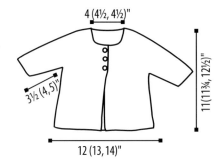

4 (4½, 4½)"
11 (11¾, 12½)"
3½ (4, 5)"
12 (13, 14)"

Sizes 6 (12, 18) months. Shown in size 6 months.
Finished measurements Chest (buttoned) 24 (26, 28)". Length 11 (11¾, 12½)".
Yarns 2 balls sport weight bouclé (each 1¾oz/50g, approx 136yd/125m) in Green multi (A); 2 balls in Brown (B). 2 balls eyelash yarn (each .88oz/20g, approx 84yd/78m) in Blue multi (C).
Needles One pair size 6 (4mm) needles, *or size to obtain gauge.*
Extras Stitch markers and holders. Size F/5 (4mm) crochet hook. Three ⅝" buttons.
Gauge 22 sts and 32 rows to 4" (10cm) over rev St st using size 6 (4mm) needles and A.

INTERMEDIATE

EDITOR'S NOTE   This garment is worked from back neck to armhole. Sleeves are worked separately, then joined to back and fronts and sweater is completed in one piece.

Eyelet pat (multiple of 2 sts plus 1)

Rows 1 and 5 (RS) Knit.

Rows 2, 4, 6, 7, and 8 Purl.

Row 3 K1, p1, *yo, p2tog, rep from* to last st, end k1.

Rep rows 1-8 for eyelet pat.

Back

Cast on 55 sts. P 1 row. Work rows 1-8 of eyelet pat a total of 5 times. Place all sts on hold.

Sleeves

Cast on 35 sts. K 5 rows. **Next (eyelet) row** (RS) K2, *yo, k2tog, rep from* to last st, k1. K 2 rows and inc 6 sts evenly across 2nd row—41 sts. Work rows 4-8 of eyelet pat once, then work rows 1-8 a total of 4 times, AT SAME TIME, inc 1 st each side of row 6 a total of 4 times—49 sts. Cut yarn and place all sts on hold.

Make a 2nd sleeve and do not cut yarn at end of final row 8. Turn.

Join sleeves to back: Next row (RS) Bind off 25 sts, k to last st and knit it tog with first st of back, k across back to last st and knit it tog with first st of other sleeve, k to end of sleeve. Turn. **Next row** (WS) Bind off 25 sts, p across—101 sts.

Body

Next row (RS) K1, [p2tog, yo] 9 times, [p1, yo] 8 times, p1, [yo, p2tog] 23 times, [yo, p1] 8 times, [yo, p2tog] 9 times, k1—117 sts. Work eyelet pat rows 4-8, then rows 1-2.

Next row (RS) K1, [p2tog, yo] 11 times, [p1, yo] 8 times, p1, [yo, p2tog] 27 times, [yo, p1] 8 times, [yo, p2tog] 11 times, k1—133 sts. Work pat rows 4-8, then rows 1-2.

Next row (RS) K1, [p2tog, yo] 13 times, [p1, yo] 8 times, p1, [yo, p2tog] 31 times, [yo, p1] 8 times, [yo, p2tog] 13 times, k1—149 sts. Work pat rows 4-8, then rows 1-2.

Next row (RS) K1, [p2tog, yo] 15 times, [p1, yo] 8 times, p1, [yo, p2tog] 35 times, [yo, p 1] 8 times, [yo, p2tog] 15 times, k1—165 sts. **Pat row 4** Purl. **Pat row 5** Bind off 5 sts, k to end. **Pat row 6** Bind off 5 sts, purl to end. Work pat rows 7-8, then 1-2, AT SAME TIME, dec 1 st each side on rows 7, 8 and 1—149 sts.

Next row (RS) K1, [p2tog, yo] 13 times, [p1, yo] 8 times, p1, [yo, p2tog] 39 times, [yo, p1] 8 times, [yo, p2tog] 13 times,

I have two sons, aged six and twelve. They are not keen on hand-knit sweaters, so I knit for my friend's granddaughters. I had several ideas for the contest, but the baby sweater was the only one I actually completed—so many ideas, so little time! I was intrigued by the idea of making a sweater with non-traditional shaping and this was the result.

I always have too many projects on the go, knitting as well as sewing and needlepoint. My family lives surrounded by chaotic stashes of wool and fabric! Kids' clothes are fast to knit and offer a change from some of the more complicated adult sweaters. Knitting for children should be colorful, comfortable and easy to care for.

This is a tip that I have always wanted to share: use a hair grip (bobby pin) for holding stitches when doing cables. It works for all thicknesses of yarn and the stitches never slip off!

Size 6 months.

Finished measurements Chest (buttoned) 20".
Length 10".

Yarns 4 balls worsted weight yarn (each 1¾oz/50g, approx 110yd/100m) in Green.

Needles One pair size 7 (4.5mm) needles, *or size to obtain gauge.*

Extras Stitch holders. Four ½" buttons. 1½ yds of ⅜" ribbon.

Gauge 21 sts and 28 rows to 4" (10cm) over St st using size 7 (4.5mm) needles.

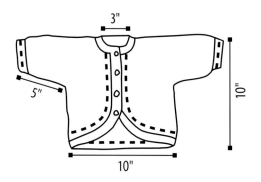

k1—165 sts. Work pat rows 4-8 then rows 1-2, then k 2 rows.

Eyelet row K1, [yo, k2tog] 15 times, [yo, k1] 9 times, [yo, k2tog] 21 times, yo, k1, yo, [k2tog, yo] 21 times, [k1, yo] 9 times, [k2tog, yo] 15 times, k1—185 sts. K 3 rows.

Buttonhole row On first 30 sts (for buttons on right front) or on last 30 sts (for buttons on left front) work as foll: *k2tog, yo, k8; rep from* twice. K 2 rows. Bind off all sts loosely.

Finishing

Block piece lightly. Sew bound-off sleeve sts to back armhole. Sew shoulder seams using approx 3½" of back cast-on edge each side. With RS facing, pick up and k approx 51 sts around neck. K 4 rows, working 1 buttonhole (k3, yo, k2tog) at beg of 2nd row. Bind off all sts loosely. Weave ribbon through eyelet rows on sleeves and body. Sew buttons on.

Carolina's Sweater

ANDREA A. WONG
REYNOLDSBURG, OHIO

EXPERIENCED

When I was 7 years old, I already had 3 dreams for my life: 1) to learn how to knit (I used to watch my mother knitting for hours); 2) to be a knitwear designer; 3) to have a daughter. My first dream came true in that same year. Since then I've been knitting non-stop. Designing Carolina's baby sweater was having my other two dreams come true: my daughter Carolina was born in 1994 and this was the first sweater, among many, that I've knitted for her. I hope you enjoy knitting it and making your dreams come true.

EDITOR'S NOTE This garment is worked in one piece from side to side.

Right Front

Cast on 65 sts. K 10 rows. Work arrowhead lace pat at lower edge and beg short rows as foll:

Row 1 (WS) [Yo, k2tog] 5 times, yo, p to last 15 sts. Turn, leaving remaining sts unworked. **Row 2** (RS) K to last 3 sts, p3. Turn.
Row 3 [Yo, k2tog] 5 times, yo, p to last 7 sts. Turn. **Row 4** P8, k to last 3 sts, p3. Turn.
Row 5 [Yo, k2tog] 5 times, yo, p to end. Turn. **Row 6** Purl all sts.
Rows 7-12 Rep rows 1-6.
Row 13 [Yo, k2tog] 6 times, p to last 15 sts. Turn. **Row 14** K to last 3 sts, p1, k2tog. Turn.
Row 15 [Yo, k2tog] 6 times, p to last 7 sts. Turn. **Row 16** P8, k to last 3 sts, p1, k2tog. Turn.
Row 17 [Yo, k2tog] 6 times, p to end. Turn. **Row 18** P to last 2 sts, k2tog. Turn.
Rows 19-24 Rep rows 13-18.
Rep rows 1-24 once more, then work rows 1-23 once. **Next row** P25 sts and place rem sts on hold.

Sleeves

Onto same needle, cast on 43 sts for sleeve—68 sts. Turn. **Row 1** (WS) P to last 15 sts. Turn. **Row 2** K to last 8 sts. Turn.
Row 3 P to last 7 sts. Turn. **Row 4** P8, k to last 8 sts, p8. Turn. **Row 5** P to end. Turn. **Row 6** P all sts. Turn. Rep last 6 rows 13 times more, then work rows 1-4 once. **Next row** (WS) Bind off 43 sts, p to end. **Join sleeve to front: Next row** P25, then p across sts on hold from body to last 2 sts, k2tog.—65 sts.

Back

Work rows 1-24 of arrowhead lace pat 5 times more, then work rows 1-23 once. **Next row** P25 sts and place rem sts on hold. Work 2nd sleeve as for first. Join 2nd sleeve to back.

Left Front

Rep 24 rows of arrowhead lace pat 3 times more. K 5 rows. **Next (buttonhole) row** (RS) K4, k2tog, yo, *k9, k2tog, yo; rep from* 3 times more, k to end. K 4 rows. Bind off all sts.

Finishing

Block piece. With RS facing, pick up and k 80 sts around neck edge. **Rows 1 and 3** Purl. **Row 2** K1, *k1, yo, k2tog, rep from* across, end k1. Bind off all sts. Sew sleeves seams Sew buttons on. Weave ribbon through eyelets at neck edge.

Size Newborn.
Measurements
Chest (buttoned) 19".
Length 10".
Yarn 3 balls fingering weight yarn (each 1¾oz/50g approx 225yd/203m) in Cream.
Needles Size 2 (2.75mm) needles, *or size to obtain gauge.*
Extras Stitch holders. Five ¼" buttons. Approx 6" of ¼" ribbon.
Gauge 32 sts and 40 rows to 4" (10cm) over St st using size 2 (2.75mm) needles.

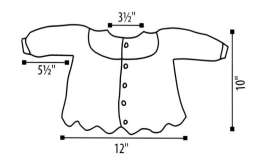

ADVANCED BEGINNER

Back

With MC, cast on 59 (63, 67) sts. **Rows 1, 3 and 5** (WS) *P3, k1; rep from*, end p3. **Rows 2 and 4** *K3, p1; rep from*, end k3. K 1 row and inc 1 (2, 3) sts evenly across—60 (65, 70) sts. Cont in St st (k on RS, p on WS) until piece measures 13 (15, 16)" from beg. Place all sts on hold.

Front

Work as for back until piece measures 9 (11, 12)" from beg, end with a WS row. **Beg Chart: Rows 1 and 3** (RS) Beg with first st and work 10-st rep across, and **for size 2 only,** work sts 11-15. **Rows 2 and 4 For size 2 only,** work sts 15-11, **for all sizes,** work 10-st rep across. Cont in St st with MC only until piece measures 10½ (12½, 13½)" from beg, end with a WS row.

Shape neck

Next row (RS) K22 (24, 25), place next 16 (17, 20) sts on hold, join a 2nd ball of yarn and k to end. Working both sides at same time, dec 1 st at each neck edge every RS row 5 times—17 (19, 20) sts each side. Work even until piece measures same as back to shoulder. Place all sts on hold.

Sleeves

With MC, cast on 35 (39, 43) sts. **Rows 1, 3 and 5** (WS) *P3, k1; rep from*, end p3. **Rows 2 and 4** *K3, p1; rep from*, end k3. Beg with a k row, work in St st, AT SAME TIME, inc 1 st each side every 4th row 10 (11, 11) times—55 (61, 65) sts. Work even until piece measures 9 (10, 11)" from beg. Bind off all sts.

Finishing

Block pieces. K shoulders tog using 3-needle bind-off.

Neck

With RS facing, circular needle and MC, beg at shoulder edge and pick up and k approx 60 (66, 74) sts evenly around neck, including sts on hold at back neck. Place marker, join and k 7 rnds. Bind off all sts loosely. Using photo as guide, work French knots (see pg. 70) with red.
Place markers 5½ (6, 6½)" down from shoulders on front and back. Sew top of sleeves between markers. Sew side and sleeve seams.

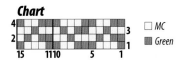

Chart

4							3
2							1
15	11	10		5		1	

☐ MC
▪ Green

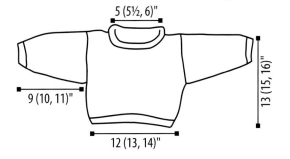

5 (5½, 6)"
9 (10, 11)"
13 (15, 16)"
12 (13, 14)"

For me, the joy of knitting is in handling a good yarn and spending my time wisely creating a useful, beautiful garment. This sweater for my granddaughter, Alaina, has simple lines, a simple pattern, in durable yarn for easy care. Holiday themes are so much fun to do. Used discreetly, they can celebrate the entire season and not just be worn for a few days.

Size 1 (2, 4) yrs. Shown in size 1.
Measurements Chest 24 (26, 28)". Length 13 (15, 16)".
Yarns 5 (6, 7) balls worsted weight yarn (each 1¾oz/50g, approx 110yd/100m) in White (MC). Small amounts in Green and Red.
Needles Size 8 (5mm) needles, *or size to obtain gauge.* Size 6 (4mm) circular needle, 16"/40cm, for neckband.
Extras Stitch holders and markers.
Gauge 20 sts and 28 rows to 4" (10cm) over St st using size 8 (5mm) needles.

What are little boys made of?

KIDS CONTEST

What are little boys made of?

Snips and snails,

And puppy dog tails,

That's what little boys are made of!

What are little girls made of?

Sugar and spice,

And everything nice,

That's what little girls are made of!

Everyday

Volkswagen Vest

INTERMEDIATE

EDITOR'S NOTE This vest is worked in one piece to the armhole, then divided into fronts and back. Use separate balls for large areas of color. Remember to twist yarns on WS to avoid holes. Stripes are worked so that yarn ends are evenly distributed on both sides.

Body
With size 4 circular needle and MC, cast on 132 (144, 160, 176) sts. Work 10 rows in k1, p1 rib. Change to size 6 circular needle and red. **Next row** (RS) K33 (36, 40, 44), place marker for side seam, k66 (72, 80, 88), place 2nd marker for side seam, k to end. **Next row** With red, purl. Push work to beg of needle so that purl side is facing you. With yellow, p 1 row, then k 1 row. Push work to beg of needle so that k side is facing you. With blue, k 1 row, then p 1 row. In same way, cont to alternate beg of rows and work 2 rows green, then 2 rows white. **Beg charts: Row 1** K3 (4, 6, 8) MC, work 28 sts of Chart A, k4 (8, 12, 17) MC, work 28 sts of Chart B, k6 (8, 12, 14) MC, work 28 sts of Chart C, k4 (8, 12, 17) MC, work 28 sts of Chart D, end k3 (4, 6, 8) MC. Work to top of charts. With MC, work even in St st until piece measures 6½ (7½, 8½, 9)" from beg, end with a WS row.

Divide for fronts and back
Next row (RS) *K to 3 sts before marker, bind off 6 sts; rep from* once, k to end—30 (33, 37, 41) sts for each front and 60 (66, 74, 82) sts for back. Turn and p30 (33, 37, 41); place rem sts on hold. Turn.

Left Front
Next row (RS) K1, ssk (underarm), k to last 3 sts, k2tog, k1 (neck edge)—28 (31, 35, 39) sts. **Next row** Purl. In same way, dec 1 st at underarm 1 (1, 2, 3) times more, AT SAME TIME, *dec 1 st at neck edge every 4th row once, every other row once; rep from* 5 (6, 7, 7) times more. Work even on rem 15 (16, 17, 20) sts until armhole measures 5½ (6½, 6½, 7)". Place all sts on hold.

Right Front
Sl sts to needle, ready to beg a WS row. Join yarn and p 1 row. **Next row** (RS) K1, ssk (neck edge), k to last 3 sts, k2tog, k1 (underarm)—28 (31, 35, 39) sts. Shape armhole and neck as for left front. Work even until armhole measures same as left front to shoulder. Place all sts on hold.

Back
Sl sts to needle, ready to beg a WS row. Join yarn and p 1 row. **Next row** (RS) K1, ssk, k to last 3 sts, k2tog, k1. Dec 1 st each side every other row 1 (1, 2, 3) times more. Work even on 56 (62, 68, 74) sts until armhole measures same as fronts to shoulder. Place all sts on hold.

Finishing
Block piece. Join shoulders using 3-needle bind-off. Place rem 26 (30, 34, 34) sts of back neck on hold. Place 4 (4, 5, 5) markers for buttonholes on left front (for boys) or right front (for girls).

Buttonband
With RS facing, size 4 circular needle and MC, beg at lower edge of right front and pick up and k approx 180 (200, 214, 228) sts evenly around fronts and neck edge, including sts on hold at back neck. Work 5 rows in k1, p1 rib, working buttonholes on row 3 at markers as foll: yo, work 2 tog.

Armbands
With RS facing, size 4 circular needle and MC, beg at underarm and pick up and k approx 72 (84, 84, 90) sts evenly around. Work 4 rows in k1, p1 rib. Bind off.
Sew armband seam. Sew buttons on.

"I like to make a 2-stitch, 1-row buttonhole as follows: Work in pattern to buttonhole location. Slip 2 stitches knitwise to right-hand needle. *Pass the first stitch over the 2nd stitch and off the right-hand needle. Slip 1 more stitch knitwise to right-hand needle and repeat from*. Cast on 2 stitches using backward loop method (or turn and cable cast on 2 stitches). Continue pattern."

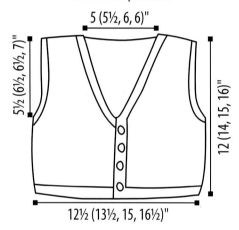

5 (5½, 6, 6)"

5½ (6½, 6½, 7)"

12 (14, 15, 16)"

12½ (13½, 15, 16½)"

Sizes 1 (2, 4, 6). Shown in size 2.

Measurements Chest (buttoned) 25 (27, 30, 33)". Length 12 (14, 15, 16)".

Yarn 2 (3, 3, 4) balls sport weight yarn (1¾oz/50g, approx 136yd/125m) in Black (MC). 1 ball each in Red, Yellow, Blue, Green and White.

Needles Size 6 (4mm) circular needle, 24"/60cm, *or size to obtain gauge.* Size 4 (3.5mm) circular needle, 24"/60cm.

Extras Stitch markers. Yarn bobbins. 4 (4, 5, 5) 'car' buttons or plain buttons in colors to match cars.

Gauge 22 sts and 30 rows to 4" (10cm) in St st using size 6 (4mm) needles and MC.

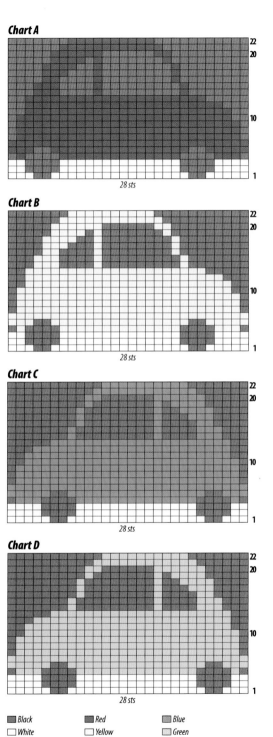

Chart A

22
20

10

1

28 sts

Chart B

22
20

10

1

28 sts

Chart C

22
20

10

1

28 sts

Chart D

22
20

10

1

28 sts

■ Black   ■ Red   ■ Blue
□ White   □ Yellow   □ Green

Let's Do the Twist

INTERMEDIATE

Evidently Joyce got off to a good start when her mother taught her to knit at the age of nine. She knits, designs, writes about knitting and is an active member of her local guild.

Sizes 2 (4, 6, 8, 10). Shown in size 6.

Measurements Pullover Chest 26 (29, 32, 35, 38)". Length 15 (16½, 18, 20, 22)". **Cardigan** Chest (buttoned) 29½ (33, 36, 39, 41½)". Length 15 (16½, 18, 20, 22)".

Yarn Pullover 3 (5, 7, 9, 11) balls worsted weight yarn (each 1¾oz/50g, approx 110yd/100m) balls in Solid color (MC) and 4 (6, 8, 10, 11) in Variegated color (CC).

Cardigan 5 (7, 9, 11, 13) balls worsted weight yarn (each 1¾oz/50g, approx 110yd/100m) balls in Solid color (MC) and 4 (6, 8, 10, 11) in Variegated color (CC).

Needles Sizes 6 and 8 (4 and 5mm) needles, *or size to obtain gauge.* **For pullover,** size 6 circular needle, 16" (40cm) long.

Extras Stitch holders and markers. **For cardigan,** five ⅝" buttons.

Gauge 20 sts and 40 rows to 4" (10cm) in garter st using size 8 (5mm) needles. 22 sts and 40 rows to 4" (10cm) in k6, RT cable pat using size 8 (5mm) needles.

Right Twist (RT) K2tog, do not sl off needle, k first st again, sl both sts off needle.

PULLOVER

Back

With smaller needles and CC, cast on 72 (80, 88, 96, 104) sts. Work 2" in k1, p1 rib. Change to larger needles. **Beg pat: Row 1** (RS) With CC, k3, *sl 2 with yarn in back (wyib), k6; rep from* to last 5 sts, end sl 2 wyib, k3. **Row 2** (WS) With CC, k3, *sl 2 with yarn in front (wyif), k6; rep from* to last 5 sts, end sl 2 wyif, k3. **Row 3** With MC, k3, *RT, k6; rep from* to last 5 sts, end RT, k3. **Row 4** With MC, k3, *p2, k6; rep from* to last 5 sts, end p2, k3. Rep rows 1-4 until piece measures 15 (16½, 18, 20, 22)" from beg. Bind off all sts.

Front

Work as for back until piece measures 12½ (13½, 15, 17, 19)" from beg, end with a WS row.

Shape neck

Next row (RS) Work 26 (28, 32, 35, 38) sts, join a 2nd ball of yarn and bind off 20 (24, 24, 26, 28) sts, work to end. **Next row** (WS) Working with 2 balls of yarn, work across both sides in pat. Cont pat and dec 1 st at each neck edge every RS row 5 times. Work even on rem 21 (23, 27, 30, 33) sts each side until piece measures same as back to shoulder. Bind off all sts.

Sleeves

With smaller needles and CC, cast on 38 (40, 44, 46, 48) sts. Work 2" in k1, p1 rib and inc 2 (0, 4, 2, 0) sts across last row—40 (40, 48, 48, 48) sts. Change to larger needles. Beg with row 1, work rows 1-4 of pat as for back, AT SAME TIME, inc 1 st each side (working incs into k6, RT pat) every 4th row 10 (11, 3, 0, 0) times, every 6th row 3 (5, 12, 15, 20) times—66 (72, 78, 78, 88) sts. Work even until piece measures 9 (10, 11, 13, 15)" from beg. Bind off all sts.

Finishing

Block pieces. Sew shoulder seams.

Neckband

With RS facing, circular needle and CC, beg at right shoulder seam and pick up and k74 (78, 78, 82, 86) sts evenly around neck edge. Place marker, join and work 2" in k1, p1 rib. Bind off loosely. Fold neckband and tack to WS.

Place markers 6 (6½, 7, 7, 8)" down from shoulders on front and back. Sew top of sleeves between markers. Sew side and sleeve seams.

CARDIGAN

Back

With smaller needles and MC, cast on 80 (88, 96, 104, 112) sts. Work 2" in k1, p1 rib. Change to larger needles. **Foundation row 1** (RS) With CC, knit. **Foundation row 2** (WS) With CC, k3, *sl 2 with yarn in front (wyif), k6; rep from* to last 5 sts, end sl 2 wyif, k3. **Beg pat: Row 1** (RS) With MC, k3, *RT, k6; rep from* to last 5 sts, end RT, k3. **Row 2** With MC, k3, *p2, k6; rep from* to last 5 sts, end p2, k3. **Row 3** With CC, k3, *sl 2 wyib, k6; rep from* to last 5 sts, end sl 2 wyib, k3. **Row 4** With CC, k3, *sl 2 with yarn in front (wyif), k6; rep from* to last 5 sts, end sl 2 wyif, k3. Rep rows 1-4 until piece measures 15 (16½, 18, 20, 22)" from beg. Bind off all sts.

Left Front

With smaller needles and MC, cast on 40 (44, 48, 52, 56) sts. Work 2" in k1, p1 rib. Change to larger needles. **Foundation row 1** (RS) With CC, knit. **Foundation row 2** With CC, k3, *sl 2 wyif, k6; rep from* to last 5 (9, 5, 9, 5) sts, end sl 2 wyif, k3 (7, 3, 7, 3). **Row 1** With MC, k3 (7, 3, 7, 3), *RT, k6; rep from* to last 5 sts, end RT, k3. **Row 2** With MC, k3, *p2, k6; rep

from* to last 5 (9, 5, 9, 5) sts, end p2, k3 (7, 3, 7, 3). **Row 3** With CC, k3 (7, 3, 7, 3), *sl 2 wyib, k6; rep from* to last 5 sts, end sl 2 wyib, k3. **Row 4** With CC, k3, *sl 2 wyif, k6; rep from* to last 5 (9, 5, 9, 5) sts, end sl 2 wyif, k3 (7, 3, 7, 3). Rep rows 1-4 until piece measures 12½ (13½, 15, 16½, 18½)" from beg, end with a RS row.

Shape neck

Next row (WS) Bind off 9 (10, 10, 11, 11) sts, cont pat to end. Cont pat and dec 1 st at neck edge every RS row 5 times. Work even on rem 26 (29, 33, 36, 40) sts until piece measures same as back to shoulder. Bind off all sts.

Right Front

Cast on and work 2" in k1, p1 rib as for left front. Change to larger needles. **Foundation row 1** (RS) With CC, knit. **Foundation row 2** With CC, k3 (7, 3, 7, 3), *sl 2 wyif, k6; rep from* to last 5 sts, end sl 2 wyif, k3. **Row 1** With MC, k3, *RT, k6; rep from* to last 5 (9, 5, 9, 5) sts, end RT, k3 (7, 3, 7, 3). **Row 2** With MC, k3 (7, 3, 7, 3), *p2, k6; rep from* to last 5 sts, end p2, k3. **Row 3** With CC, k3, *sl 2 wyib, k6; rep from* to last 5 (9, 5, 9, 5) sts, end sl 2 wyib, k3 (7, 3, 7, 3). **Row 4** With CC, k3 (7, 3, 7, 3), *sl 2 wyif, k6; rep from* to last 5 sts, end sl 2 wyif, k3. Rep rows 1-4 until piece measures 12½ (13½, 15, 16½, 18½)" from beg, end with a WS row. Shape neck as for left front, binding off at beg of RS row. When piece measures same as back to shoulder, bind off all sts.

Sleeves

With smaller needles and MC, cast on 42 (44, 46, 48, 48) sts. Work 2" in k1, p1 rib and inc 6 (4, 2, 0, 0) sts evenly across last row—48 sts. Change to larger needles. **Foundation row 1** (RS) With CC, knit. **Foundation row 2** With CC, k3, *sl 2 wyif, k6; rep from* to last 5 sts, end sl 2 wyif, k3. **Row 1** With MC, k3, *RT, k6; rep from* to last 5 sts, end RT, k3. **Row 2** With MC, k3, *p2, k6; rep from* to last 5 sts, end p2, k3. **Row 3** With CC, k3, *sl 2 wyib, k6; rep from* to last 5 sts, end sl 2 wyib, k3. **Row 4** With CC, k3, *sl 2 wyif, k6; rep from* to last 5 sts, end sl 2 wyif, k3. Rep rows 1-4, AT SAME TIME, inc 1 st each side (working incs into k6, RT pat) every 4th row 10 (13, 15, 16, 20) times, every 6th row 5 (5, 5, 7, 8) times—78 (84, 88, 94, 104) sts. Work even in pat until piece measures 10 (11, 12, 14, 16)" from beg. Bind off all sts.

Finishing

Block pieces. Sew shoulder seams.

Neckband

With RS facing, smaller needles and MC, beg at right front neck and pick up and k approx 73 (77, 81, 85, 87) sts evenly around to left front neck. Work 1" in k1, p1 rib. Bind off all sts.

Buttonband

With RS facing, smaller needles and MC, pick up and k approx 64 (68, 72, 76, 80) sts evenly along left front (for girls) or right front (for boys). Work 6 rows in k1, p1 rib. Bind off all sts. Place 5 markers on band, the first and last approx 1" from lower edge and neck edge and 3 others spaced evenly between.

Buttonhole band

Work as for buttonband and work buttonholes as foll: on row 3 of ribbing, bind off 2 sts opposite each marker. On row 4, cast on 2 sts over bound-off sts of previous row. Place markers 7 (7½, 8, 8½, 9½)" down from shoulders on front and back. Sew top of sleeves between markers. Sew side and sleeve seams. Sew buttons on.

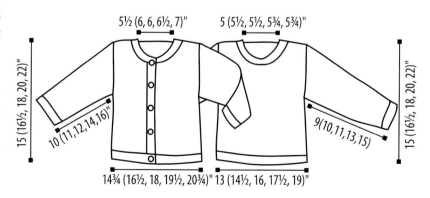

Confetti Pullover

INTERMEDIATE

When I knit for kids,
I focus on easy care and fit
and like to use machine-washable
wools and blends.
I use lots of colors in an allover design
because it's hard to see
the inevitable dirt and drool.
Most kids hate having tight things
pulled over their heads.
Often I shape a low/wide V-neck,
then knit a shawl collar
(which could be extended into a hood);
it overlaps in front.

Sizes 2 (4, 6, 8, 10). Shown in size 2.

Measurements Chest 27 (30, 33, 36, 39)". Length 15 (16, 17, 19, 22)".

Yarn 2 (3, 3, 4, 5) balls worsted weight yarn (each 1¾oz/50g, approx 110yd/100m) each in Purple, Red, Yellow, Blue and Teal.

Needles One pair each sizes 7 and 8 (4.5 and 5mm) needles, *or size to obtain gauge.*

Extras Stitch holders and markers. One ½" button.

Gauge 20 sts and 28 rows to 4" (10cm) in St st using size 8 (5mm) needles. 21 sts and 42 rows to 4" (10cm) in Multi-Color Ladder pat using size 8 (5mm) needles.

Multi-Color Ladders pat (multiple of 4 sts plus 3)
Row 1 (RS) K3, *sl 1 with yarn in back, k3; rep from* across. **Row 2** K3, *sl 1 with yarn in front, k3; rep from* across. **Row 3** K1, sl 1, *k3, sl 1 with yarn in back; rep from* to last st, end k1. **Row 4** P1, sl 1 with yarn in front, *p3, sl 1 with yarn in front; rep from* to last st, end p1. **Color sequence** *2 rows each red, yellow, blue, teal, purple; rep from* for color sequence.

Back

With smaller needles and purple, cast on 71 (79, 87, 95, 103) sts. K 11 (11, 15, 19, 19) rows. Change to larger needles. Work in Multi-Color Ladders pat and color sequence as foll: With red, work rows 1-2. With yellow, work rows 3-4. With blue, work rows 1-2. With teal, work rows 3-4. With purple, work rows 1-2. Cont pat in color sequence (working rows 3-4 with red, then rows 1-2 with yellow, etc.) until piece measures 15 (16, 17, 19, 22)" from beg. Bind off all sts.

Front

With smaller needles and purple, cast on as for back and k 9 (9, 13, 15, 15) rows. **Next row** (RS) K16 (20, 22, 26, 28), k next 39 (39, 43, 43, 47) sts and place them on hold, k to end. **Next row** K16 (20, 22, 26, 28), cast on 39 (39, 43, 43, 47) sts, k to end. Work in Multi-Color Ladders pat as for back until piece measures 11 (12, 13, 15, 18)" from beg, end with a WS row.

Shape placket and neck

Next row (RS) Cont pat, work 33 (37, 41, 45, 49) sts, join a 2nd ball of yarn and bind off 5 sts, work to end. Working both sides at same time, work even for 1½". Bind off 2 (2, 2, 3, 3) sts from each neck edge 3 times. Dec 1 st each side of neck every other row 6 (7, 7, 5, 5) times. Work even on rem 21 (24, 28, 31, 35) sts each side until piece measures same as back to shoulders. Bind off all sts.

Pocket

Sl 39 (39, 43, 43, 47) sts on hold at lower edge of front to larger needles, ready to work a WS row. **Next row** (WS) With purple, knit. Work Multi-Color Ladders pat in color sequence (working rows 1-2 with red, rows 3-4 with yellow, etc.) until piece measures 2 (2½, 2½, 2½, 2½)" from beg, end with a WS row.

Shape sides

Cont pat, dec 1 st each side every 4th row 2 (2, 1, 0, 0) times, every 6th row 6 (6, 7, 8, 8) times. Work even on rem 23 (23, 27, 27, 31) sts until piece measures 6 (6½, 6½, 7½, 7½)" from beg. Bind off all sts.

Edgings

With RS facing, smaller needles and red, pick up and k approx 22 (22, 24, 26, 28) sts along each shaped side edge. K 5 rows. Bind off.

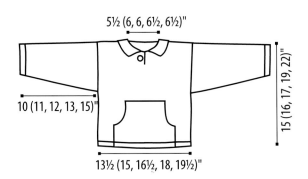

5½ (6, 6, 6½, 6½)"

15 (16, 17, 19, 22)"

10 (11, 12, 13, 15)"

13½ (15, 16½, 18, 19½)"

Sleeves

With smaller needles and purple, cast on 39 (43, 43, 47, 47) sts. K 11 (11, 15, 19, 19) rows. Change to larger needles. Work Multi-Color Ladders pat in color sequence, AT SAME TIME, inc 1 st each side (working incs into pat) every 6th row 1 (5, 15, 0, 15) times, every 8th row 10 (8, 0, 13, 3) times. Work even on 61 (69, 73, 73, 83) sts until piece measures 10 (11, 12, 13, 15)" from beg. Bind off all sts.

Finishing

Block pieces. Tack top of pocket to front, lining up colors so pats match. Tack sides of pocket to front, then tack cast-on sts at lower edge of front to inside of pocket. Sew shoulder seams.

Placket

With RS facing, smaller needles and purple, pick up and k approx 10 sts along left front (for girls) or right front (for boys). K 8 rows. Bind off. In same way, pick up on rem side, working a buttonhole (yo, k2tog) in middle of placket. Sew lower edges of placket to front. Sew button opposite buttonhole.

Collar

With RS facing, smaller needles and purple, beg at right neck edge after placket and pick up and k approx 65 (71, 71, 77, 77) sts evenly around to left neck edge, not including top of placket. K every row until collar measures 2 (2½, 2½, 3, 3)" from beg. Bind off all sts loosely. Place markers 6 (6½, 7, 7, 8)" down from shoulders on front and back. Sew top of sleeves between markers. Sew side and sleeve seams.

Emily's Sweater

ADVANCED BEGINNER

My granddaughter was seven when she helped me dye the yarn and knit this sweater. With eight skeins of undyed worsted-weight yarn that I had re-skeined into 24 hanks, Emily and I got to work. We used my 1.5-quart, 2-quart, and 3-quart saucepans and grape, orange, raspberry, cherry, lemon and lime Kool-Aid (three packages and one-half cup of white vinegar per pot). We'd stir the concoction until it was well mixed, add the small hank, boil until the water turned clear and carefully (with tongs) get the hot yarn outside to dry. Then back to the pot for the next color. This is not a cheap way to dye wool; but it was great fun. As for the knitting, it turned out that Emily did not yet enjoy fine-muscle work, so she knit only two small rectangles. I added more to make her work a part of the sweater. For the basic pattern, I copied her favorite sweatshirt.

Sizes 2 (4, 6, 8, 10). Shown in size 8.

Measurements Chest 26 (30, 32, 36, 38)". Length 15 (16½, 18, 20, 23)".

Yarn 5 (7, 8, 9, 10) balls Aran weight yarn (each 1¾oz/50g, approx 88yd/80m) in Variegated Rust/Brown (MC). Approx 2 balls in Brown (A) and 1 ball each in Cream (B) and Red (used for floating rectangles).

Needles One pair each sizes 7 and 9 (4.5 and 5.5mm) needles, *or size to obtain gauge.*

Extras Stitch markers.

Gauge 16 sts and 24 rows to 4" (10cm) in St st using size 9 (5.5mm) needles and MC.

EDITOR'S NOTE Take a close look at the photo. Notice that there are small (between 6 to 12 sts) rectangles of color randomly placed throughout the sweater. As you work through the horizontal stripe pat, insert a rectangle when the spirit moves you. Use 2 to 3 yard strands of yarn. Work in garter st (k every row) so the rectangles will have a different texture.

The horizontal stripe pat is established in the back. Carry the yarn not in use loosely across on the WS, twisting colors to prevent holes. Follow the first set of stripes to get the hang of it, then feel free to experiment with 'fleck' placement. Stagger them (as explained in the pat) or line them up. Put more of them in or leave some of them out. You can also make the MC stripes wider or narrower as you wish. When you work the sleeves, work the fleck pat evenly into the sts that you have. As you increase, you'll have more 'flecks' along the row. Feel free to 'fleck' the back, front and two sleeves differently. Treat this pattern as a canvas for your painterly instincts!

Back

With smaller needles and A, cast on 53 (61, 65, 73, 77) sts. Work 1½ (2, 2, 2½, 2½)" in k1, p1 rib. Change to larger needles. Work in St st (k on RS, p on WS) and stripe pat as foll:

Row 1 (RS) K2 (3, 2, 0, 2) A, *k1 B, k5 A; rep from* across, end k1 B, k2 (3, 2, 0, 2) A.

Row 2 With A, purl.

Row 3 K5 (6, 5, 3, 5) A, *k1 MC, k5 A; rep from* across, end k1 MC, k5 (6, 5, 3, 5) A.

Rows 4-8 With MC, beg with a p row and work in St st (k on RS, p on WS).

Row 9 Rep row 1 using MC for A and B for B.

Rows 10-14 Rep rows 4-8.

Rows 15-18 With B, beg with a k row and work in St st.

Rows 19-22 With MC, beg with a k row and work in St st.

Row 23 Rep row 3, using MC and A.

Rows 24-28 Rep rows 4-8.

Rows 29-30 With A, work 2 rows in St st.

Row 31 With A and B, rep row 1.

Row 32 With A, purl.

Cont in stripe pat, *working 2" in MC with a row of colored flecks in the middle, 4 rows B, 1½" in MC with a row of colored flecks in the middle, 4 rows A; rep from*. Stagger the flecks of A on MC or B on A or line them up vertically as desired. Work even until piece measures 15 (16½, 18, 20, 23)" from beg. Bind off all sts.

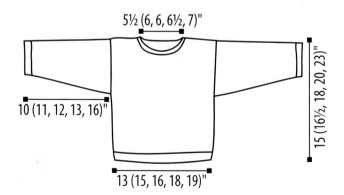

5½ (6, 6, 6½, 7)"

10 (11, 12, 13, 16)"

13 (15, 16, 18, 19)"

15 (16½, 18, 20, 23)"

Front

Work as for back until piece measures 12½ (14, 15, 17, 20)" from beg, end with a RS row.

Shape neck

Next row (RS) Work 18 (21, 23, 26, 27) sts, join a 2nd ball of yarn and bind off 17 (19, 19, 21, 23) sts, work to end. Working both sides at same time, dec 1 st at each neck edge every RS row 3 times. Work even on rem 15 (18, 20, 23, 24) sts each side until piece measures same as back to shoulder. Bind off all sts.

Sleeves

With smaller needles and A, cast on 30 (32, 34, 36, 36) sts. Work 1½ (2, 2, 2½, 2½)" in k1, p1 rib. Change to larger needles. Work in St st and horizontal stripe pat as for body, AT SAME TIME, inc 1 st each side every 4th row 4 (6, 7, 9, 6) times, every 6th row 5 (4, 4, 3, 8) times—48 (52, 56, 60, 64) sts. Work even until piece measures 10 (11, 12, 13, 16)" from beg. Bind off all sts.

Finishing

Block pieces. Sew right shoulder.

Neckband

With RS facing, smaller needles and A, beg at left front shoulder and pick up and k approx 62 (66, 70, 74, 78) sts evenly around neck. Work 1" in k1, p1 rib. Bind off loosely.

Sew left shoulder, including neckband. Place markers 6 (6½, 7, 7½, 8)" down from shoulders on front and back. Sew top of sleeves between markers. Sew side and sleeve seams.

St. George and the Dragon

Almost all of my knitting is for my children and my husband: colorful picture sweaters for the children and subdued Norwegian sweaters for Leif. Levin and I had seen a puppet show, so St. George and the Dragon became his 4th-birthday sweater.

EDITOR'S NOTE To get a finished chest measurement of approx 36", use larger needles and worsted weight yarn and get a gauge of 5 sts to 1". For a 40" finished chest, use worsted weight yarn and even larger needles and work the chart at a gauge of 4½ sts to 1". Look the chart over carefully and mark the places where you can add length. Working a 2nd band motif at lower edge (chart rows 1-10) would add approx 1½". Add a bit more sky and perhaps a 2nd shoulder motif. 2 rows here and there can easily add up to another inch.

Back

With smaller needles and red, cast on 86 sts. **Work hem** Beg with a p row, work 7 rows in St st. With purple, k 2 rows and inc 4 sts evenly across 2nd row—90 sts. Change to larger needles. Beg with row 1 (RS), work to top of Chart for Back, shaping armhole and neck as indicated.

Front

Cast on and work hem as for Back. Work rows 1-108 of Chart for Front, shaping armhole and neck as indicated.

Right Sleeve

With smaller needles and purple, cast on 40 sts. **Work hem** Beg with a p row, work 7 rows in k1, p1 rib. K 2 rows and inc 6 sts evenly across 2nd row—46 sts. Change to larger needles. Beg with row 1 (RS), work to top of Chart for Right Sleeve, shaping as indicated.

Left Sleeve

Cast on and work hem as for right sleeve. Work rows 1-86 of Chart for Left Sleeve, shaping as indicated.

Finishing

Block pieces. Sew shoulder seams.

Neckband

With RS facing, circular needle and purple, pick up and k 81 sts evenly around neckline. Work 9-st rep of rnd 1 of Chart for Neck around, taking care to center cross at center front neck. Work through rnd 10. With purple, k 1 rnd, then p 1 rnd. K 9 rnds. Bind off loosely.

Set in sleeves. Sew side and sleeve seams. Fold hems at hemline ridge and sew to WS.

Size 3-5 yrs.

Finished measurements Chest 31". Length 16".

Yarns Sport weight yarn (1¾oz/50g, approx 136yd/125m): see main color key and Note, pg. 35.

Needles One pair each sizes 3 and 5 (3.25 and 3.75mm), *or size to obtain gauge.* Size 3 (3.25mm) circular needle, 16" (40cm) long.

Extras Bobbins.

Gauge 22 sts and 28 rows to 4" (10cm) over St st using size 5 (3.75mm) needles.

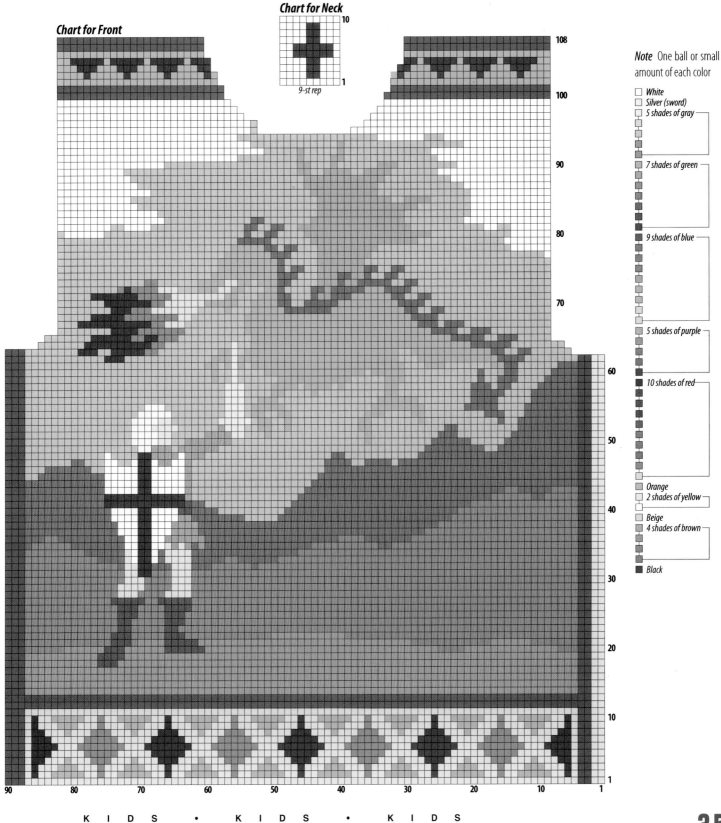

Chart for Front

Chart for Neck

9-st rep

Note One ball or small amount of each color

☐ White
☐ Silver (sword)
☐ 5 shades of gray
☐ 7 shades of green
☐ 9 shades of blue
☐ 5 shades of purple
☐ 10 shades of red
☐ Orange
☐ 2 shades of yellow
☐ Beige
☐ 4 shades of brown
■ Black

Chart for Back

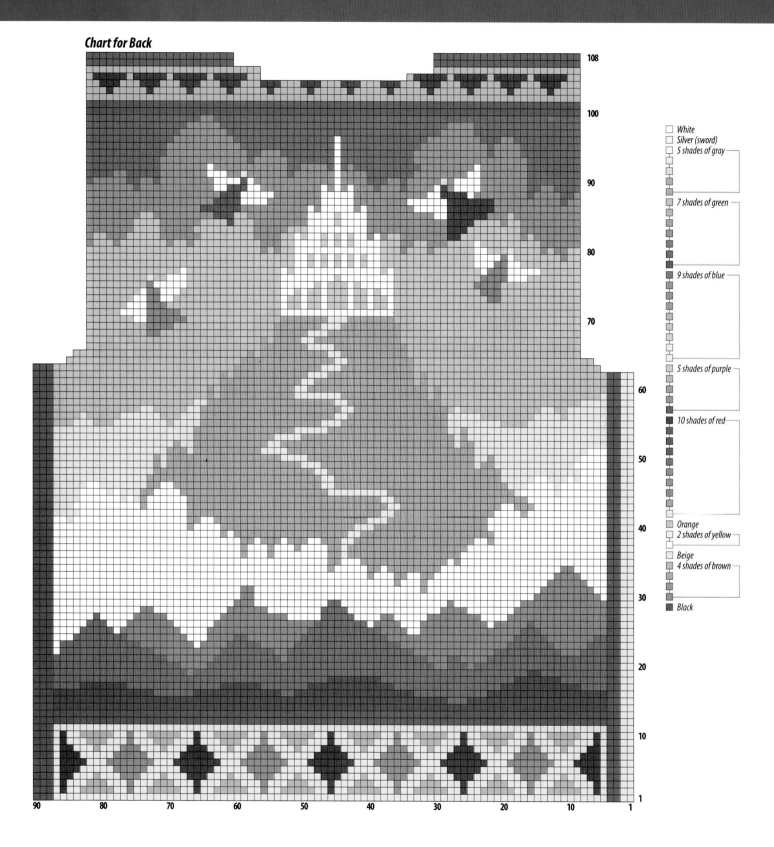

White
Silver (sword)
5 shades of gray

7 shades of green

9 shades of blue

5 shades of purple

10 shades of red

Orange
2 shades of yellow

Beige
4 shades of brown

Black

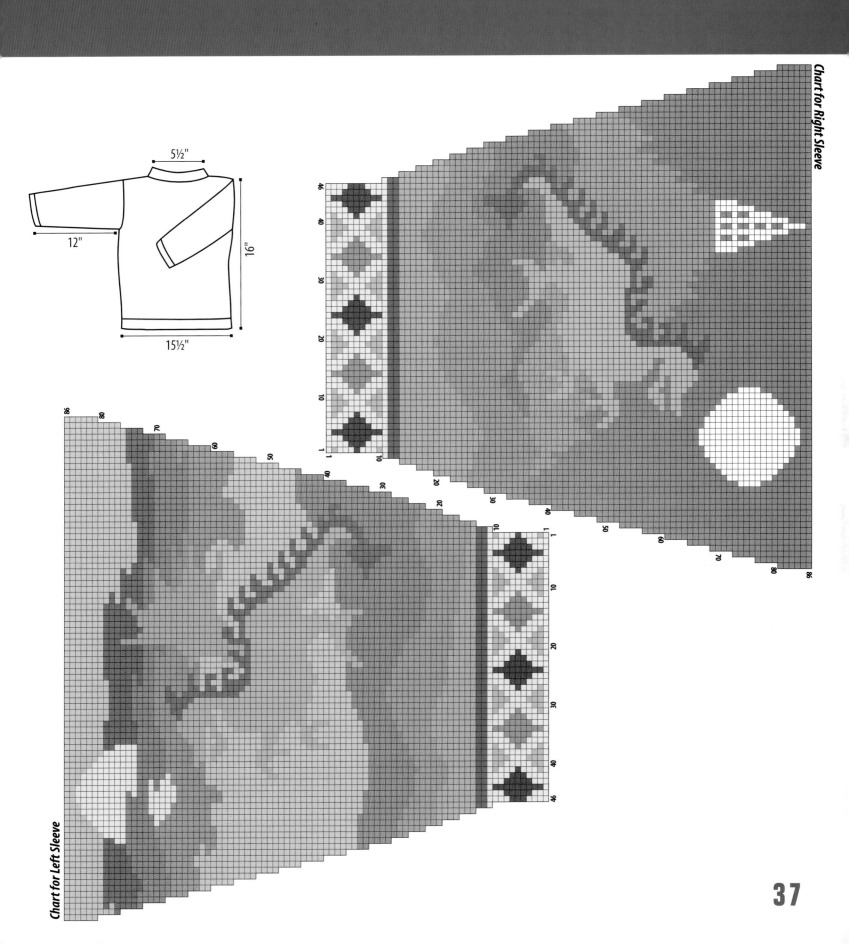

Chart for Left Sleeve

5½"

12"

16"

15½"

BEGINNER

Back

With larger needles and CC, cast on 52 (58, 64) sts. Work 8 rows in k1, p1 rib. **Work stripe pat** *With MC, beg with a k row and work 6 rows in St st. With CC, work 2 rows in St st. Rep from* 2 (2, 3) times more. With MC, work in St st until piece measures 12 (14, 16)" from beg, end with a WS row. Bind off 15 (17, 20) sts at beg of next 2 rows. Place rem 22 (24, 24) sts on hold.

Right Front

With larger needles and CC, cast on 26 (29, 32) sts. Work 8 rows in k1, p1 rib. Work stripe pat as for back, then cont in St st with MC until piece measures 9½ (11½, 13)" from beg, end with a WS row.

Shape Neck

Next Row (RS) Bind off 6 (7, 7) sts, work to end. **Next row** K1, ssk, k to end. **Next row** Purl. Rep last 2 rows 4 times more—15 (17, 20) sts. Work even until piece measures same as back to shoulder. Bind off all sts.

Left Front

Work as for right front until piece measures 9½ (11½, 13)" from beg, end with a RS row.

Shape Neck

Next Row (WS) Bind off 6 (7, 7) sts, work to end. **Next row** K to last 3 sts, k2tog, k1. **Next row** Purl. Rep last 2 rows 4 times more—15 (17, 20) sts. Work even until piece measures same as back to shoulder. Bind off all sts.

Sleeves

With larger needles and CC, cast on 32 (32, 36) sts. Work 8 rows in k1, p1 rib. With MC, work in St st, AT SAME TIME, inc 1 st each side every 6th row 7 (10, 10) times—46 (52, 56) sts. Work even until piece measures 10 (11, 12)" from beg. Bind off all sts.

Finishing

Block pieces. Sew shoulder seams.

Right front band With RS facing, smaller needles and CC, beg at lower right front edge and pick up and k40 (48, 56) sts evenly to neck edge. Beg first row with p1, work 7 rows in k1, p1 rib. Bind off all sts in rib.

Left front band Work to correspond to right front band, beg at neck edge and pick up to lower edge.

Neckband With RS facing, smaller needles and CC, beg at edge of right front band and pick up and k 22 (23, 25) sts along neck, k across 22 (24, 24) sts on hold at back neck and dec 1 st at center, pick up and k 22 (23, 25) sts along left

Sizes 2 (4, 6) yrs. Shown in size 4.

Finished measurements Chest 26 (29, 32)". Length 12 (14, 16)".

Yarns 4 (4, 5) balls Aran weight yarn (each 1¾ oz/50g, approx 88yd/80m) in Lavender (MC). 1 (1, 2) balls in Lime (CC).

Needles One pair each sizes 8 and 9 (5 and 5.5mm) needles, *or size to obtain gauge.*

Extras Stitch holder. One ⅞" (22mm) flower button.

Gauge 16 sts and 24 rows to 4" (10cm) over St st using size 9 (5.5mm) needles.

I started knitting for my first grandchild,
Celia, as soon as she was born.
When she was almost two
I knit this cardigan out of some purple
yarn I had in my stash. Having always
liked the green and purple combination,
I thought that lime would give the
sweater a kick. Celia thought so too—
this was her favorite sweater
until she outgrew it.
So my only comment about knitting for
kids is that you really can't knit a
garment too big—they'll grow into it
and out of it all too soon.

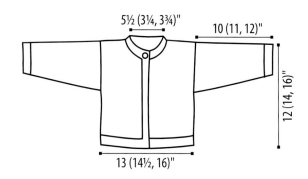

front neck—65 (69, 73) sts. **Row 1** Beg with p1, work in k1, p1 rib. **Row 2** Rib 3, bind off 2 sts, rib to end. **Row 3** Rib to bound-off sts, cast on 2 sts, rib to end. **Rows 4-7** Work in rib. Bind off all sts in rib. Sew button on. Place markers 5¾ (6½, 7)" down from shoulders on fronts and back. Sew top of sleeves between markers. Sew side and sleeve seams.

Purple Turtles

INTERMEDIATE

When I designed this sweater, I was fascinated with combinations of red and purple and wanted to use these colors together in a sweater. Then I came across purple turtle beads and decided to create the effect of purple turtles. I used a variation of the coin stitch in Barbara Walker's *A Treasury of Knitting Patterns.* In the body of this sweater I used purple turtles (or coins) on a red background. For playfulness and fun, the left sleeve has red turtles on a purple background and the right sleeve has red and purple stripes in stockinette stitch. All of the ribbings are different striped combinations of red and purple.

Sizes 1 (2, 4, 6, 8). Shown in size 4.

Measurements Chest (buttoned) 24 (26, 29½, 33, 36½)". Length 13 (15, 16½, 17½, 18)".

Yarn 4 (4, 5, 6, 6) balls worsted weight yarn (each 1¾oz/50g, approx 110yd/100m) each in Purple (MC) and Red (CC).

Needles One pair each sizes 6 and 8 (4 and 5mm) needles, *or size to obtain gauge.* Size 6 (4mm) circular needle, 24"/60cm long.

Extras Stitch markers. Five ½" buttons.

Gauge 20 sts and 28 rows to 4" (10cm) in St st using size 8 (5mm) needles and MC.
24 sts and 48 rows to 5" (13cm) in Purple Turtles pat using size 8 (5mm) needles and MC and CC.

Purple Turtles (multiple of 4 sts plus 2)
Row 1 (RS) With MC, *k3, yo, sl 1; rep from*, end k2.
Rows 2 and 4 With MC, p2, *sl 1 and the yo('s) from previous row('s), yo, p3; rep from*.
Row 3 (RS) With MC, *k3, yo, sl the yo's from previous row's and the sl 1; rep from*, end k2.
Row 5 With CC, knit, knitting sl 1 tog with yo's from previous rows.
Row 6 With CC, purl.
Row 7 With MC, k1, *yo, sl 1, k3; rep from*, end last rep k4.
Rows 8 and 10 With MC, p4, *sl 1 and the yo('s) from previous row('s), yo, p3; rep from*, end last rep p1.
Row 9 With MC, k1, *yo, sl the yo's from previous row's and the sl 1, k3; rep from*, end last rep k4.
Rows 11 and 12 Rep rows 5-6.
Rep rows 1-12 for Purple Turtles pat.

Back
With smaller needles and MC, cast on 58 (62, 70, 78, 86) sts. **Rib row 1** (WS) *P2, k2; rep from*, end p2. **Rib row 2** *K2, p2; rep from*, end k2. With CC, p 1 row, then work rib row 2. With MC, p 1 row, then work 2 rows more in rib. Change to larger needles. With CC, k 1 row, then p 1 row. Beg with row 1, work in Purple Turtles pat until piece measures 12 (14, 15½, 16½, 17)" from beg, end with a WS row.

Shape neck
Next row (RS) Cont pat, work 19 (20, 23, 27, 30) sts, join a 2nd ball of yarn and bind off 20 (22, 24, 24, 26) sts, work to end. Working both sides at same time, dec 1 st at each neck edge every RS row twice. Work even on 17 (18, 21, 25, 28) sts each side until piece measures 13 (15, 16½, 17½, 18)" from beg. Bind off all sts.

Left Front
With smaller needles and MC, cast on 26 (30, 34, 38, 42) sts. With MC and CC, work 7 rows in rib as for back. Change to larger needles. With CC, k 1 row, then p 1 row. Beg with row 1, work in Purple Turtles pat until piece measures 7½ (9, 10, 10½, 11)" from beg, end with a WS row.

Shape neck
Next row (RS) Cont pat, dec 1 st at end of this row, then every 4th row 4 (11, 12, 9, 10) times more, every 6 row 4 (0, 0, 3, 3) times. Work even on rem 17 (18, 21, 25, 28) sts each side until piece measures same as back to shoulder. Bind off all sts.

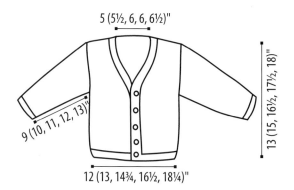

5 (5½, 6, 6, 6½)"

13 (15, 16½, 17½, 18)"

9 (10, 11, 12, 13)"

12 (13, 14¾, 16½, 18¼)"

Right Front

Work as for left front. Reverse neck shaping by working neck decs at beg of RS rows.

Right Sleeve

With smaller needles and CC, cast on 34 (38, 38, 42, 42) sts. Work 2 rows in rib as for back. With MC, p 1 row, then work 1 row rib. With CC, p 1 row, then work 2 rows rib. Change to larger needles. With MC, k 1 row, then p 1 row. Beg with row 1, work in Purple Turtles pat (using CC for rows 1-4 and 7-10 and MC for rows 5-6 and 11-12), AT SAME TIME, inc 1 st each side (working sts into Purple Turtles pat) every 6th row 2 (2, 3, 3, 0) times, every 8th row 7 (8, 9, 10, 13) times. Work even on 52 (58, 62, 68, 68) sts until piece measures 9 (10, 11, 12, 13)" from beg. Bind off all sts.

Left Sleeve

With smaller needles and CC, cast on and work 1 row rib as for right sleeve. *With MC, k 1 row, then work 1 row rib. Rep from * with CC, then with MC. Change to larger needles and St st, working 4 rows CC, 4 rows MC, AT SAME TIME, inc 1 st each side every 4th row 9 (6, 10, 8, 5) times, every 6th row 2 (5, 4, 6, 9) times. Work even on 56 (60, 66, 70, 70) sts until piece measures same as right sleeve from beg. Bind off all sts.

Finishing

Block pieces. Sew shoulder seams. Place 5 markers for buttonholes (on left front for boys, on right front for girls), the first and last approx ½" from lower edge and beg of V-neck shaping and 3 others spaced evenly between.

Frontbands

With RS facing, circular needle and MC, beg at lower edge of right front and pick up and k approx 71 (80, 89, 93, 96) sts evenly to shoulder, 24 (26, 28, 28, 30) sts along back neck, 71 (80, 89, 93, 96) sts evenly to lower left front edge—166 (186, 206, 214, 222) sts. **Rib rows 1 and 2** Work as for back. **Row 3** With CC, purl. **Rib row 4** With CC, work in rib and work buttonholes at markers as foll: yo, work 2 tog. **Rib rows 5 and 6** With CC, work in rib. **Row7** With MC, purl. **Rib row 8** With MC, work in rib and bind off at same time.

Place markers 5½ (6, 6½, 7, 7)" down from shoulders on front and back. Sew top of sleeves between markers. Sew side and sleeve seams. Sew buttons on.

Red, White and Blue!

INTERMEDIATE

EDITOR'S NOTE This is a roomy, over-sized cardigan. You can easily duplicate stitch the year of your choice on the pocket and 'USA' on the sleeves. Remember to twist colors on WS to prevent holes. Although the front bands are crocheted, they can be picked up and knit. Use 1 size smaller needles and work in k1, p1 rib. Make buttonholes by working yo, k2tog. The lower edges of body and sleeves will roll. Measure pieces with edges flat.

Back

With red, cast on 70 (74, 78, 84) sts. Beg with a p row, work 7 rows in St st. **Beg color pat: Row 1** (RS) K4 (0, 4, 2) red, k8 (0, 0, 8) white, *k8 red, k8 white; rep from* 2 (3, 3, 3) times, end k10 red. **Row 2** Purl across in colors as established. **Row 3** Knit across, moving colors 2 sts over to the left. **Row 4** Rep row 2. Rep rows 3-4 until piece measures 9 (10, 11, 13)" from beg, end with a WS row.

Shape armhole

Bind off 5 sts at the beg of the next 2 rows—60 (64, 68, 74) sts. Change to navy. **Beg Chart 1: Row 1** (RS) K2 (0, 2, 1) navy, work 8-st rep across, end k2 (0, 2, 1) navy. Cont chart pat as established, working 8-row rep, until armhole measures 7 (7½, 8, 9)". Bind off 15 (16, 18, 20) sts at beg of next 2 rows. Place rem 30 (32, 32, 34) sts on hold.

Left Front

With red, cast on 34 (36, 38, 40) sts. Beg with a p row, work even in St st until piece measures 8½ (9½, 10½, 12½)" from beg, end with a WS row. Work stripe pat as foll: *2 rows navy, 2 rows white; rep from* for stripe pat, AT SAME TIME, when piece measures same as back to underarm, shape underarm at beg of RS row as for back—29 (31, 33, 35) sts. Work even in stripe pat until armhole measures 4½ (5, 5½, 6½)", end with a RS row.

Shape neck

Next row (WS) Bind off 10 sts, work to end. Dec 1 st at neck edge every other row 4 (5, 5, 5) times. When armhole measures same as back to shoulder, bind off rem 15 (16, 18, 20) sts.

Right Front

Shape piece and work in color pat as foll: With red, cast on 34 (36, 38, 40) sts. Beg with a p row, work in St st and stripe pat as foll: 13 rows red; 10 rows each white, then navy; 9 rows each red, white, then navy; 8 rows each red, white, then navy; 7 rows each red, white, then navy; AT SAME TIME, when piece measures same as back to armhole, shape armhole at beg of WS row. When armhole measures same as left front to neck, shape neck at beg of RS row. Complete as for left front, rep 7 row stripes of red, white and navy if necessary.

Left Sleeve

Note Beg Flag chart when piece is 5 (6, 6, 7)" from beg (centering chart). Work to top of chart, then cont sleeve with white only.

With white, cast on 36 (36, 40, 40) sts. Beg with a p row, work in St st, AT SAME TIME, inc 1 st each side every other row 2 (0, 0, 6) times, every 4th row 12 (16, 16, 15) times—64 (68, 72, 82) sts. Work even until piece measures 12 (13, 14, 16)" from beg. Bind off all sts.

Right Sleeve

With red, cast on 36 (36, 40, 40) sts and work incs

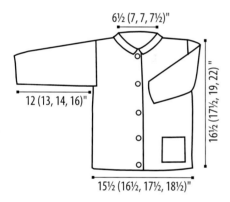

6½ (7, 7, 7½)"

12 (13, 14, 16)"

16½ (17½, 19, 22)"

15½ (16½, 17½, 18½)"

Sizes 4 (6, 8, 10). Shown in size 8.

Finished measurements Chest (buttoned) 31 (33, 35, 37)". Length 16 (17½, 19, 22)".

Yarns 3 (4, 4, 5) balls worsted weight yarn (each 1¾oz/50g, approx 110yd/100m) each in Red, White and Navy.

Needles Size 8 (5mm) needles, *or size to obtain gauge.*

Extras Stitch holders and markers. Bobbins. Size F/5 (3¾mm) crochet hook. Five ⅝" buttons.

Gauge 18 sts and 24 rows to 4" (10cm) over St st using size 8 (5mm) needles.

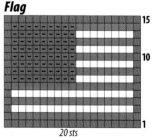

Flag

20 sts

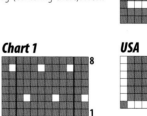

Chart 1

8-st rep

■ Red in St st
□ White in St st
■ Navy in St st
▬ Navy in rev St st

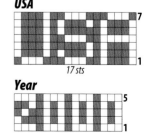

USA

17 sts

Year

15 sts

as for left sleeve. Beg with a p row, work 11 rows in St st. *On next row, center chart and work 7 rows of USA chart in navy. With red, work 5 rows in St st. Rep from*, alternating white and navy lettering until there are 3 navy USA's. Complete incs and when piece measures same as left sleeve, bind off all sts.

Pocket

With navy, cast on 15 sts. Beg with a p row, work 5 rows in St st. Work 5 rows of Year chart. With navy, work 6 rows more in St st. Work 4 rows in k1, p1 rib. Bind off.

Finishing

Block pieces. Sew shoulder seams.

Buttonband

With RS facing, navy and crochet hook, join yarn to left front neck edge and work 1 row sc evenly to neck edge. Work 2 rows more in sc in front lps only. Fasten off. Place 5 markers for buttons, the first and last 1" from lower edge and neck edge and 3 others spaced evenly between.

Buttonhole band

Work as for buttonband, beg at right lower edge, working buttonholes on row 2 opposite markers as foll: ch 2, skip 2 sc. Fasten off.

Collar

With RS facing and navy, beg at right front neck and pick up and k 19 (21, 21, 23) sts to shoulder, k sts on hold at back neck and dec 2 (3, 3, 3) sts evenly across, pick up and k 19 (21, 21, 23) sts to left front neck. Beg with a p row, work in St st as foll: 3 rows navy, 2 rows white, 6 rows red. Do not bind off. With crochet hook, work 1 row sc across all open sts. Work 1 row sc in front lps only. Fasten off.

Set in sleeves. Sew side and sleeve seams, reversing the 6 rows at lower edges of sleeves and body so seam doesn't show when rolled. Sew buttons on. Sew pocket to left front. Tack down front edges of collar.

Hiawatha

EXPERIENCED

A lot of my ideas for sweaters come from stories the children love. My daughter Jerina had memorized part of *Hiawatha* in school, so that became her 9th-birthday sweater.

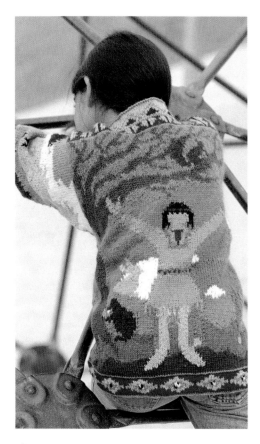

Sizes 6-8 yrs.

Finished measurements Chest 38". Length 22½".

Yarns Sport weight yarn (1¾oz/50g, 136yd/125m): see main color key and Note, pg. 41.

Needles One pair each sizes 3 and 5 (3.25 and 3.75mm) needles, *or size to obtain gauge*. Size 3 (3.25mm) circular needle, 16" (40cm) long.

Extras Bobbins.

Gauge 22 sts and 28 rows to 4" (10cm) over St st using size 5 (3.75mm) needles.

EDITOR'S NOTE To get a finished chest measurement of approx 35", use smaller needles and get a gauge of 6 sts to 1". For a 42½" finished chest, use larger needles and worsted weight yarn and work the chart at a gauge of 5 sts to 1". Add length by working a 2nd band motif at lower edge (chart rows 1-10). You could also work more solid 'ground' beneath Hiawatha's feet. Add armhole depth by working more of the tree motif (back) or more sky above the bird (front). To subtract length, work fewer rows when convenient. For example, shorten Hiawatha's legs by 2 rows, the skirt by 2 rows, the sky above the head for 2 rows and the sky beneath the shoulders by 4 rows—overall, you've taken out approx 1½".

Back

With smaller needles and teal, cast on 100 sts. **Work hem** Beg with a p row, work 7 rows in St st. K 2 rows and inc 6 sts evenly across first row—106 sts. Change to larger needles. Beg with row 1 (RS), work to top of Chart for Back, shaping armhole and neck as indicated.

Front

Cast on and work hem as for Back. Work rows 1-152 of Chart for Front, shaping armhole and neck as indicated.

Sleeves

With smaller needles and teal, cast on 46 sts. **Work hem** Beg with a p row, work 7 rows in St st. K 2 rows and inc 6 sts evenly across 2nd row—52 sts. Change to larger needles. Beg with a RS row, work Chart for Right Sleeve, shaping as indicated. Make 2nd sleeve, working Chart for Left Sleeve.

Finishing

Block pieces. Sew shoulder seams.

Neckband

With RS facing, circular needle and teal, pick up and k 90 sts evenly around neckline. Work 10-st rep of rnd 1 of Chart for Neck, taking care to center motif at front neck. Work through chart rnd 8. With teal, k 1 rnd, p 1 rnd, then k 9 rnds. Bind off loosely. Set in sleeves. Sew side and sleeve seams. Fold hems at ridge and sew to WS.

Chart for Front

Neck motif

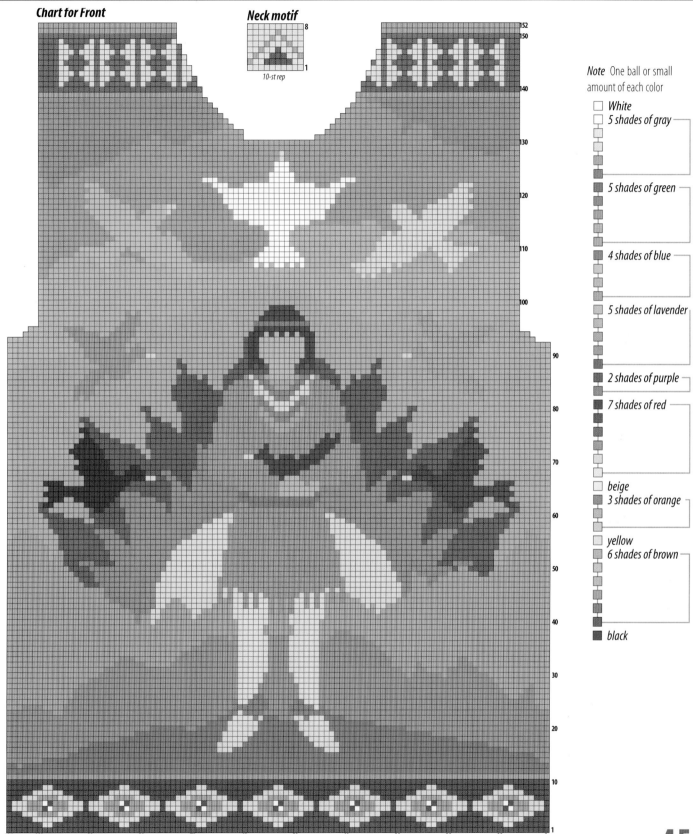

10-st rep

Note One ball or small amount of each color

☐ *White*
5 shades of gray

5 shades of green

4 shades of blue

5 shades of lavender

2 shades of purple

7 shades of red

beige
3 shades of orange

yellow
6 shades of brown

black

45

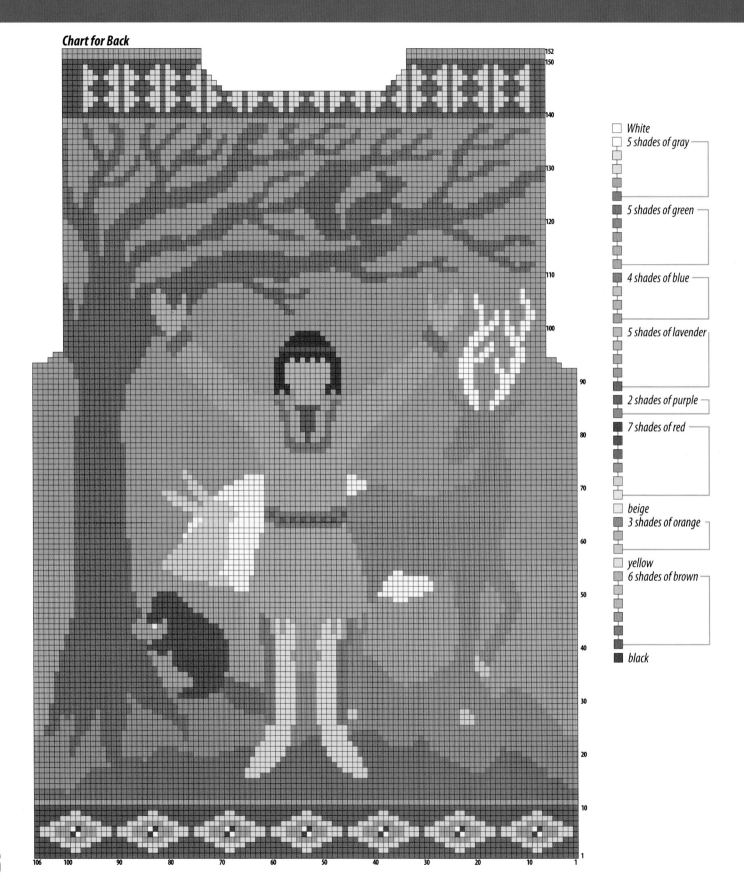

Chart for Back

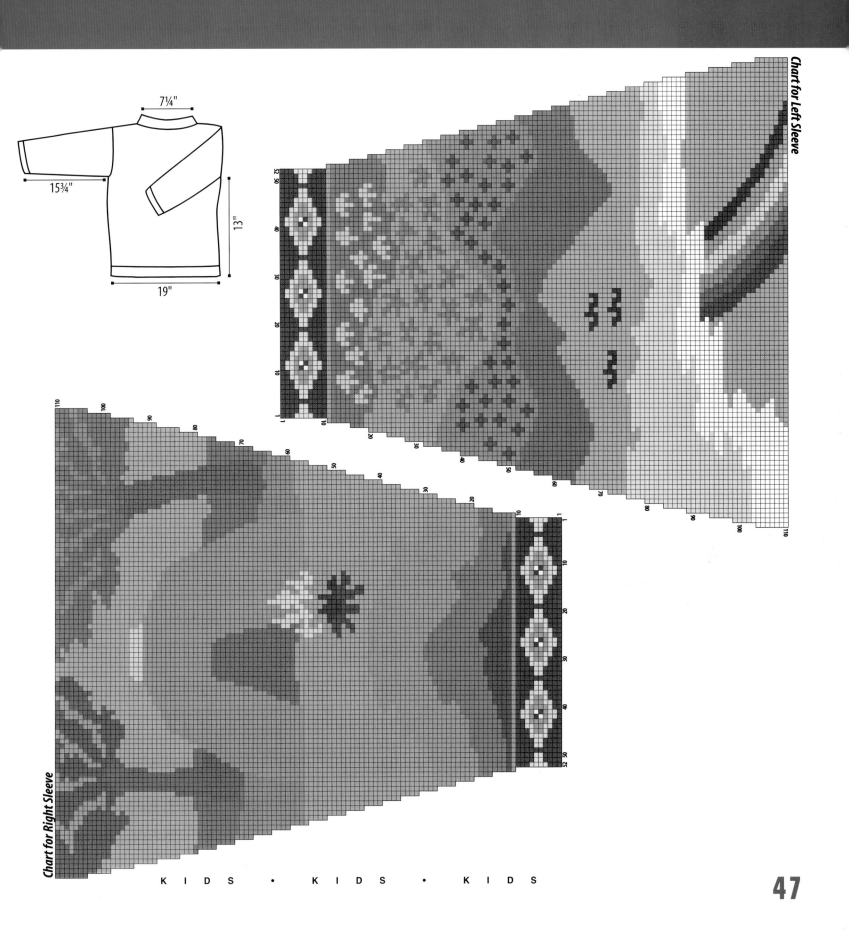

7¼"

15¾"

13"

19"

K I D S   •   K I D S   •   K I D S

Colorblock Sweater

EASY

The best part of shopping for wool is all the great colors. Yet it's so hard to choose among them. This sweater takes advantage of my limited technical knitting skills, and my inability to choose just one color! The trick is to pick three colors that are all about the same value, or "degree of darkness." They can be similar colors, but I like the combination of contrasting colors best, as in this sweater.

Size 2 (4, 6, 8, 10) years. Shown in size 6.

Measurements Chest (buttoned) 28 (30, 32, 35, 38). Length 15 (16½, 18, 20, 22)".

Materials 3 (4, 4, 5, 5) balls worsted weight yarn (each 1¾oz/50g, approx 110yd/100m) each in Raspberry (B) and Turquoise (C). 2 (3, 3, 4, 4) balls in Gold (A).

Needles One pair each sizes 6 and 8 (4 and 5mm) needles, *or size to obtain gauge.*

Extras Stitch markers. 5 (5, 6, 6, 6) ¾" buttons.

Gauge 20 sts and 28 rows to 4" over St st using size 8 (5mm) needles.

EDITOR'S NOTE Twist colors on WS to prevent holes.

Back

With smaller needles and A, cast on 70 (76, 80, 88, 96) sts. Work 2" in k1, p1 rib. Change to larger needles. **Next row** (RS) With B, k35 (38, 40, 44, 48) sts; with C, k rem 35 (38, 40, 44, 48) sts. **Next row** (WS) P in colors as established. Rep last 2 rows until piece measures 15 (16½, 18, 20, 22)" from beg. Place sts on hold.

Left Front

With smaller needles and A, cast on 32 (35, 38, 40, 45) sts. Work 2" in k1, p1 rib. Change to larger needles and B. Beg with a k row, work in St st until piece measures 12½ (14, 15, 17, 19)" from beg, end with a RS row.

Shape neck

Next row (WS) Bind off 7 (7, 8, 9, 10) sts, p across. **Next row** (RS) K to last 3 sts, k2tog, k1. **Next row** Purl. Rep last 2 rows 4 times more. Work even on rem 20 (23, 25, 26, 30) sts until piece measures same as back to shoulder. Place sts on hold.

Right Front

Cast on and work rib as for left front. Change to larger needles and C. Work in St st until piece measures 12½ (14, 15, 17, 19)" from beg, end with a WS row.

Shape neck

Next row (RS) Bind off 7 (7, 8, 9, 10) sts, k across. **Next row** (WS) Purl. **Next row** K1, ssk, k across. Rep last 2 rows 4 times more. Work even on rem 20 (23, 25, 26, 30) sts until piece measures same as back to shoulder. Place sts on hold

Left Sleeve

With smaller needles and A, cast on 38 (40, 42, 46, 46) sts. Work 2" in k1, p1 rib. Change to larger needles. **Next row** (RS) With C, k19 (20, 21, 23, 23) sts; with B, k rem 19 (20, 21, 23, 23) sts. **Next row** (WS) Purl in colors as established. Rep last 2 rows, AT SAME TIME, inc 1 st each side every 4th row 11 (13, 14, 0, 10) times, every 6th row 0 (0, 0, 12, 7) times—60 (66, 70, 70, 80) sts. Work even until piece measures 9 (10, 11, 13, 15)" from beg. Bind off all sts.

Right Sleeve

Cast on and work rib as for left sleeve. Change to larger needles. **Next row** (RS) With B, k19 (20, 21, 23, 23) sts; with C, k rem 19 (20, 21, 23, 23) sts. **Next row** (WS) Purl in colors as established. Rep last 2 rows and shape as for left sleeve. Bind off all sts.

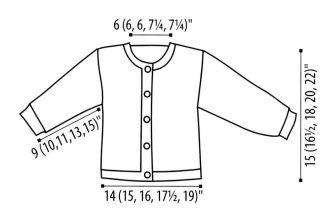

6 (6, 6, 7¼, 7¼)"

9 (10, 11, 13, 15)"

15 (16½, 18, 20, 22)"

14 (15, 16, 17½, 19)"

Finishing

Block pieces. Join shoulders using 3-needle bind-off, leaving center 30 (30, 30, 36, 36) sts on hold at back neck.

Neckband

With RS facing, smaller needles and A, beg at right front neck and pick up and k approx 22 (24, 26, 28, 28) sts to shoulder, k across sts on hold at back neck, dec to 29 (29, 29, 35, 35) sts by k2tog where B and C meet at center back, pick up and k 22 (24, 26, 28, 28) sts to left front neck—73 (77, 81, 91, 91) sts. Work 2" in k1, p1 rib. Bind off all sts loosely in rib. Fold neckband in half and sew to WS.

Buttonband

With smaller needles and A, cast on 9 sts. **Row 1** (RS) K1, [p1, k1] 4 times. **Row 2** K1, [k1, p1] 3 times, k2. Rep rows 1-2 and after a few inches, beg to sew band to left front (for girls) or right front (for boys). Work band until piece, slightly stretched, fits evenly along front to top of neckband. Bind off. Sew 5 (5, 6, 6, 6) buttons evenly along band, the first 1" from lower edge, the last in middle of neckband, and 3 (3, 4, 4, 4) others spaced evenly between.

Buttonhole band

With smaller needles and A, cast on 9 sts. **Row 1** (RS) K1, [k1, p1] 3 times, k2. **Row 2** (RS) K1, [p1, k1] 4 times. Rep last 2 rows, AT SAME TIME, work buttonholes opposite markers by working 3 sts, binding off next 2 sts, work rem sts. On next row, work 4 sts, cast on 2 sts, work rem sts. Sew band to right front (for girls) or left front (for boys), stretching slightly to fit.

Place markers 6 (6½, 7, 7, 8)" down from shoulders on front and back. Matching colors at shoulder seam, sew top of right and left sleeves to body. Sew side and sleeve seams.

I'm late, I'm late...
for a very important date!

There was nothing so very remarkable in that,

nor did Alice think it so very much

out of the way to hear the rabbit say to itself,

"Oh dear, oh dear! I shall be too late!"

Special Occasions

Easter/Party Dress

INTERMEDIATE

I learned to knit 15 years ago and knit
nothing but socks the first 2 years.
I didn't think I had the patience for
anything larger until my sister started
having babies. With no children
of my own, I am surrounded
by an extended family of 'adopted'
nieces and nephews. This design came
from one I made for my niece Willow's
new baby, Kiana.
I view all my sweaters as a bank
account for my future children.
My sister's got them neatly tucked
away, ready for the next cousins!

EDITOR'S NOTE   The directions are written for the buttons to be on the back. We photographed the dress with the buttons in front. As you can see, it's pretty either way!

STITCH GLOSSARY

Right Twist (RT) K2tog, do not sl off needle, k first st again, sl both sts off needle.

Left Twist (LT) K 2nd st on left-hand needle through the back loop, do not sl off needle, k first st through the front loop, sl both sts off needle.

Slip stitch pat in rnds (sl sts with yarn in back; mult of 6 sts)
Rnds 1-2 With CC, *k2, sl 2, k2; rep from* around. **Rnd 3** With MC, *k1, RT, LT, k1; rep from* around. **Rnd 4** With MC, knit. Rnds 5-6 With CC, *sl 1, k4, sl 1; rep from* around. **Rnd 7** With MC, *LT, k2, RT; rep from* around. **Rnd 8** With MC, knit. Rep rnds 1-8 for Slip st pat in rnds.

Slip stitch pat in rows (sl sts with yarn in back on RS rows, with yarn in front on WS rows; mult of 6 sts)
Row 1 (RS) With CC, *k2, sl 2, k2; rep from*. **Row 2** (WS) With CC, * p2, sl 2, p2; rep from*. **Row 3** With MC, *k1, RT, LT, k1; rep from*. **Row 4** With MC, purl. **Row 5** With CC, *sl 1, k4, sl 1; rep from*. **Row 6** With CC, *sl 1, p4, sl 1; rep from*. Row 7 With MC, *LT, k2, RT; rep from*. **Row 8** With MC, purl. Rep rows 1-8 for Slip st pat in rows.

Body (worked in one piece to yoke)
With larger crochet hook and 2 strands of CC held tog, cast on using chain cast-on as foll: ch 200 (216). With circular needle and one strand MC, insert needle into back lps of crochet ch and pick up and k 1 st in each ch—200 (216) sts. Being careful not to twist sts, place marker, join and [k7, sl 1] 25 (27) times. Rep last rnd 3 times more. With MC, cont in St st until piece measures 10¼(12¾)" from beg, end at marker. **Dec row** *K1, k2tog; rep from* around, end k2 (0)—134 (144) sts. K 1 rnd and dec 2 (0) sts evenly spaced—132 (144) sts. Work Slip st pat in rnds for 2½ (3½)", end with rnd 8 at marker.

Divide for Front and Back
Sl 66 (72) sts onto straight needles for Front. Place rem 66 (72) sts on hold for Back.

Front
Beg with row 1, work in Slip st pat in rows and shape armhole as foll: Bind off 5 sts at beg of next 2 rows. Dec 1 st each side every other row 3 times—50 (56) sts. Work even until armhole measures 2½ (3)", end with a WS row.

Shape neck
Next row (RS) Cont pat, work 21 (23) sts, join a 2nd ball of yarn and bind off center 8 (10) sts, work to end. Working both sides at same time, bind off from each neck edge 2 sts twice. Dec 1 st at each neck edge every other row 6 times—11 (13) sts each side. Work even until armhole measures 5 (5½)", end with a WS row. Bind off all sts.

Sizes 2 (4) yrs. Shown in size 4.

Finished measurements Chest 24 (26)". Length 18 (22)" .

Yarns 5 (6) balls worsted weight yarn (each 1¾oz/50g, approx 110yd/100m) in Pink (MC). 2 balls in Sage Green (CC).

Needles One pair size 6 (4mm) needles, *or size to obtain gauge.* Size 6 (4mm) circular needle, 24" 60cm long.

Extras Stitch markers and holders. Sizes D/3 (3mm) and H/8 (5mm) crochet hooks. Two ½" (12mm) heart-shaped buttons.

Gauge 20 sts and 28 rows to 4" (10cm) over St st using size 6 (4mm) needles.

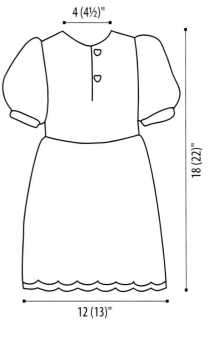

4 (4½)"

18 (22)"

12 (13)"

Back

With RS facing, sl rem 66 (72) sts onto needle and place marker 35 (38) sts in from right edge. **Divide for center back opening: Next row** (RS) Bind off 5 sts (armhole), work row 1 of Slip st pat in rows to marker, with a 2nd ball of yarn and CC, cast on 4 sts, then cont pat to end. Working both sides at same time, shape armhole as for front and at 1½ (2)", work first buttonhole on right back: On RS row, work to last 4 sts, bind off 2 sts, work rem 2 sts. On next row, work 2 sts, cast on 2 sts, work to end—27 (30) sts each side. In same way, work 2nd buttonhole when armhole is 3½ (4)". Work even until armhole is 4 (4½)", end with a WS row.

Shape neck

Bind off 12 (13) sts from each neck edge once. Dec 1 st at each neck edge every row 4 times—11 (13) sts each side. Work even until back measures same as front to shoulder. Bind off all sts.

Sleeves

With straight needles and MC, cast on 42 (48) sts. Beg with a p row, work 5 rows in St st. Beg with row 1, work 10 rows in Slip st pat. Fasten off CC. **Next (inc) row** (RS) With MC, k2 (0), *k into front and back of next st, k1; rep from* across—62 (72) sts. Work even in St st until piece measures 2½ (3¼)" from beg, end with a WS row.

Shape cap

Bind off 5 sts at beg of next 2 rows. Dec 1 st each side every other row 13 (16) times—26 (30) sts. **Next (dec) row** (RS) K3 (5), [k2tog, k4] 3 times, k2tog, k3 (5)—22 (26) sts. Work one row even. Bind off all sts.

Finishing

Block pieces. Sew shoulder seams. Sew cast-on sts at center back in place. With RS facing, MC and smaller crochet hook, work 1 row sc around entire neck and back opening. Sew buttons on. Set in sleeves. Sew sleeve seams.

Pañuelo #2

EXPERIENCED

EDITOR'S NOTE
This garment is knit in one piece from side to side. Make a good-sized swatch to insure that you are getting the correct row gauge. Twist colors on WS to prevent holes. If desired, cast on for body using an invisible cast-on. Instead of binding off body sts at opposite side, place them on hold. With WS facing, you can then join sides of body tog using 3-needle bind-off.

Placket insert
With larger needles and purple, cast on 17 sts. Work 5 rows in seed st. Place all sts on hold.

Right sleeve
With smaller needles and purple, cast on 46 (48, 48) sts. Work 1 (1½, 1½)" in k1, p1 rib. **Next row** (RS) *K3 white, k3 black; rep from* across, end k1 black for size 4. Work 2 rows more in St st in colors as established. With red, beg with a p row and work 3 rows in St st. Work chart pat and shape sleeve simultaneously as foll: Working 6-st rep, rep 36 rows of Chart A, working solid color stripes as foll: *Purple, green, fuchsia, purple, green, red; rep from*. AT SAME TIME, inc 1 st each side (working incs into chart pat) every 4th row 2 (7, 7) times, every 6th row 11 (8, 8) times—72 (78, 78) sts. Work even until 14 patterned stripes and 13 solid color stripes have been worked, end ready to beg a purple stripe. With purple, work 2 rows in St st and cast on 45 (48, 57) sts at end of each row for front and back. With purple, p 1 row over 162 (174, 192) sts.

Body
Work rows 7-15 of Chart A, using green as the solid stripe. With fuchsia, beg with a p row and work 6 (8, 10) rows in St st. Working row 1 as a WS row, work rows 1-5 of Chart B. With purple, beg with a k row and work 6 (8, 10) rows in St st. **Next row** (RS) Working row 1 as a RS row, work row 1 of Chart C over 50 (56, 65) sts, place marker, with purple, work seed st over next 36 sts, place 2nd marker, work Chart C over rem 76 (82, 91) sts. Work next 4 rows in colors and pats (Chart C rows 2-5) as established, working 3 buttonholes on 3rd row as foll: work to marker, seed 2 sts, [yo, work 2 tog, seed 4 sts] 3 times, work in pat to end.

Divide for neck
Place placket insert on spare needle, ready to work a RS row. **Next row** (RS) With green, k 50 (56, 65) sts, then k across 12 sts of placket insert, with purple, k across rem 5 sts of placket insert. On left-hand needle, with 2nd ball of purple, bind off 31 sts, work seed over 5 sts, with 2nd ball of green, k to end. Working both sides at same time, work 5 (7, 9) rows more (St st in

Sizes 4 (6, 8). Shown in size 4.

Sizes 4 (6, 8). Shown in size 4.

Measurements Chest 28 (30, 34)". Length 15 (16½, 18)".

Yarn 2 (3, 4) balls in sport weight yarn (each 1¾oz/50g, approx 136yd/125m) each in Purple and Black. 1 (2, 2) balls each in Yellow, White, Green, Fuchsia and Red.

Needles One pair each sizes 3 and 5 (3.25 and 3.75mm) needles, or size to obtain gauge.

Extras Stitch holders and markers. Three ⅜" buttons.

Gauge 24 sts and 32 rows to 4" (10cm) in St st using size 5 (3.75mm) needles.

This sweater was inspired by the beautiful ethnic household textiles of Guatemala, where I lived for two years. Almost all the indigenous ladies carry colorful pañuelos, or handkerchiefs, which serve any number of purposes. Knotted, they carry change or laundry or groceries; folded over the head they keep the sun off; spread in baskets they keep tortillas warm. I used mine as tablecloths, chair pads and a cat bed. The typical pañuelo is about two feet square and woven out of very brightly colored cotton, with solid stripes alternating with ikat or small repeating patterns in black and white, yellow or often orange. The fabric designs are similar to those of the corte, or wrap skirt, worn by many of the more traditional women of Guatemala. When a corte is worn, the stripes always run vertically. When I designed this sweater, I wanted the stripes to run vertically since nothing else looked quite right.

Chart A

Chart B
6-st rep

Chart C
6-st rep

■ Black
□ White
■ Purple
□ Yellow
■ Green
■ Fuchsia
■ Red

6-st rep

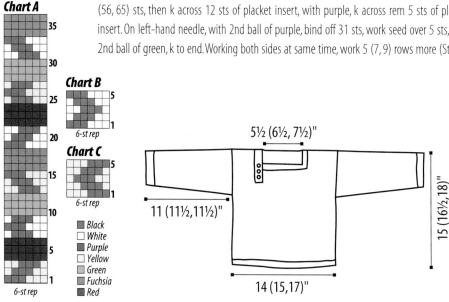

5½ (6½, 7½)"

11 (11½, 11½)"

15 (16½, 18)"

14 (15, 17)"

T E S T   K I D S   C O N -

green and seed st in purple at each neck edge). Alternate Chart B and Chart C pats and 6 (8, 10) rows of solid color as foll: 5 rows Chart B, red, 5 rows Chart C, fuchsia, 5 rows Chart B, green. **Next row** (RS) Work 62 (68, 77) sts of Chart C, row 1, with purple, work 5 sts in seed st, then cast on 14 sts, join pieces and work to end—162 (174, 192) sts. Complete Chart C, working neck and cast-on sts in seed st. Work 6 (8, 10) rows in St st with purple, 5 rows of Chart B, then 6 (8, 10) rows in St st with red. Work rows 1-9 in Chart A pat, working solid stripe in green. With purple, p 1 row. Work 2 rows more in St st and bind off 45 (48, 57) sts at beg of each row—72 (78, 78) sts.

Left sleeve

Work pats to mirror right sleeve, working solid color stripes as foll: *pink, green, purple, red, green, purple; rep from*, AT SAME TIME, dec 1 st each side every 6th row 11 (8, 8) times, every 4th row 2 (7, 7) times. Work even until 13 solid stripes have been worked after body bind-offs, end with pink 46 (48, 48) sts. **Next row** (RS) *K3 white, k3 black; rep from*. Work 2 rows more in colors as established. Change to smaller needles. With purple, work 1 (1½, 1½)" in k1, p1 rib. Bind off in rib.

Finishing

Block piece to measurements. Sew placket insert to WS. Sew buttons on. Sew side and sleeve seams.

Lower band

With circular needle and purple, pick up and k approx 168 (180, 204) sts evenly around lower edge. K 7 rnds, then work 5 rnds in seed st. Bind off in seed st.

Beribboned!

EXPERIENCED

> **EDITOR'S NOTE** Garment is knit entirely in MC yarn. Ribbon is then duplicate stitched along cables. Use photo as guide in choosing ribbon colors.

STITCH GLOSSARY

Twisted Rib (over an even number of sts)

Row 1 *K1 through the back loop (tbl), p1; rep from* across. Rep row 1 for Twisted Rib pat.

For Twisted Rib pat over an odd number of sts, end row 1 with k1 tbl. Beg next row with p1, then work row 1 across.

3/3 Right Cross (3/3RC)

Sl 3 sts to cable needle, hold to back, k3; k3 from cable needle.

Back

With smaller needles and MC, cast on 122 (130, 138) sts. Work 1" in Twisted Rib pat, end with a WS row. Change to larger needles. **Rows 1, 3, 5 and 9** (RS) P2, *k6, p2; rep from* across. **Rows 2, 4, 6, 8 and 10** K the knit sts and p the purl sts. **Row 7** P2, *3/3RC, p2; rep from* across. Rep rows 1-10 until piece measures 13 (14½, 16½)" from beg, end with a WS row. Place 40 (42, 45) sts each side on hold. Place rem sts on hold.

Right Front

With smaller needles and MC, cast on 58 (61, 66) sts. Work in Twisted Rib as for back. Change to larger needles. **Rows 1, 3, 5 and 9** (RS) K0 (3, 0), p2, *k6, p2; rep from* across. **Rows 2, 4, 6, 8 and 10** K the knit sts, p the purl sts. **Row 7** K0 (3, 0), p2, *3/3RC, p2; rep from* across. Work even in pat until piece measures 11 (12, 14)" from beg, end with a WS row.

Shape neck

Cont pat, bind off 5 sts at neck edge twice, 4 sts once. Dec 1 st at neck edge every row 4 (5, 7) times—40 (42, 45) sts. Work even in pat until piece measures same as back to shoulder, end with a WS row. Place sts on hold.

Left Front

With smaller needles and MC, cast on 58 (61, 66) sts. Work in Twisted Rib as for Back. Change to larger needles. **Rows 1, 3, 5 and 9** (RS) P2, *k6, p2; rep from* across, end k0 (3, 0). **Rows 2, 4, 6, 8 and 10** K the knit sts, p the purl sts. **Row 7** P2, *3/3RC, p2; rep from* across, end k0 (3, 0). Work even in pat to correspond to right front, reversing neck shaping.

Sleeves

With smaller needles and MC, cast on 66 (74, 74) sts. Work in Twisted Rib as for Back. Change to larger needles. **Row 1** (RS) P2, *k6, p2; rep from* across. **Row 2** K the knit sts, p the purl sts. Cont 10-row cable pat as for back, AT SAME TIME, inc 1 st each side (working incs into cable pat) every 4th row 17 (18, 20) times—100 (110, 114) sts. Work even until piece measures 9½ (10½, 12)" from beg. Bind off all sts.

It amazes me that a small garment could represent so much in my life. When I look at this sweater, I think of my festive daughter, Pilar, and my new career. Beribboned is the first garment that I have designed from beginning to end. After seeing my daughter's fascination with all the brightly colored ribbons at the sewing store, I started to formulate this sweater. Although it took some time and planning, the results made me feel eager and confident to head full steam into an industry I have always loved. Most importantly, the sweater brings a smile to my face every time I see it, just like Pilar.

Sizes 2 (4, 6) yrs. Shown in size 4.

Finished measurements Chest (buttoned) 30½ (32½, 34½)". Length 13 (14½, 16½)".

Yarns 6 (7, 8) balls sport weight yarn (each 1¾oz/50g, approx 136yd/124m) in Cream (MC).

⅛ " wide ribbon in assorted colors as foll:

Size 2 58 lengths, each approx 101"/257cm; 48 lengths, each approx 77"/196cm.

Size 4 60 lengths, each approx 112"/285cm; 52 lengths, each approx 85"/216cm .

Size 6 66 lengths, each approx 128"/325cm; 56 lengths, each approx 97"/246cm.

Needles One pair each sizes 2 and 6 (3 and 4mm) needles, *or size to obtain gauge.*

Extras Cable needle. Stitch holders and markers. Five (five, six) ⅝" (15mm) buttons.

Gauge 32 sts and 34 rows to 4" (10cm) over Cable pat using size 6 (4mm) needles.

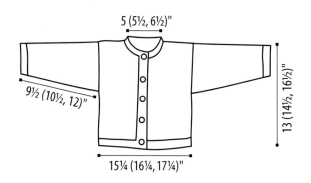

5 (5½, 6½)"

9½ (10½, 12)"

15¼ (16¼, 17¼)"

13 (14½, 16½)"

Finishing

Using 3-needle bind-off, graft shoulders tog. Using photo as guide, duplicate st CC colors along 2nd and 4th st of each cable. Use longer lengths for fronts and back, shorter lengths for sleeves.

Buttonband

With RS facing, smaller needles and MC, beg at left front neck edge and pick up and k84 (94, 106) sts evenly to lower edge. Beg with a WS row, work 8 rows in Twisted Rib pat. Bind off in rib. Using photo as guide, place 4 (4, 5) markers for buttons, the first ½" from lower edge, the last 2¼ (2½, 2¼) from upper edge and the rest spaced evenly between.

Buttonhole band

Work to correspond to buttonband, beg at right front lower edge, working buttonholes opposite markers as foll: on row 4, bind off 4 sts; on row 5, cast on 4 sts over each set of bound-off sts.

Neckband

With RS facing, smaller needles and MC, beg at right front neck and pick up and k46 (53, 58) sts evenly to shoulder, k across 42 (46, 48) sts from back holder; pick up and k46 (53, 58) sts evenly along left front neck—134 (152, 164) sts. Beg with a WS row, work 8 rows in Twisted rib, working final buttonhole (on rows 4 and 5) centered above right front band. Bind off in rib.

Place markers 6½ (7¼, 8¼)" down from shoulders on front and back. Sew top of sleeves between markers. Sew side and sleeve seams. Sew buttons on.

Vested Bears

EXPERIENCED

As the designing of this project progressed, my grandchildren would get excited trying to find new play areas for the mini bears. The bears can live in the pockets and we left openings for them when attaching the tree and seed st arm. I have a box full of these little bears that they play with on every visit. I have also turned them into pins as gifts for friends.

EDITOR'S NOTE Use larger needles for all pieces except mini-bears. Tree and pocket outlines on charts are for placement only. They do not indicate number of sts or rows.

Seed st (over any number of sts)
Row 1 *K1, p1; rep from*. Row 2 K the purl sts and p the knit sts. Rep row 2 for seed st pat.

VEST

Back

With Navy, cast on 60 sts. [P 1 row, k 1 row] twice. Work Chart for Back (p. 60), shaping neck as indicated. Bind off all sts.

Tree

With brown, cast on 18 sts. Work 5 rows in seed st. **Rows 1 and 3** (RS) Knit. **Rows 2 and 4** K2, *p2, k2; rep from*. **Row 5** K1, *k2tog, do not sl off needle, k first st, sl both sts from needle; k 2nd st through the back loop (tbl), do not sl off needle, k first st, sl both sts off needle; rep from*, end k1. **Rows 6, 8 and 10** P2, *k2, p2; rep from*. **Rows 7 and 9** Knit. **Row 11** K1, *k 2nd st tbl, do not sl off needle, k first st, sl both sts off needle; k2tog, do not sl off needle, k first st, sl both sts from needle; rep from*, end k1. **Row 12** Rep row 2. Rep rows 1–12 until piece measures 5½" from beg, end with a WS row.

Shape branches Work in seed st on first 4 sts only (leaving rem sts on hold) for approx 3½", dec 1 st on last row. Work approx 5" in I-cord on rem 3 sts. With RS facing, work seed st across next 6 sts. Work even for 1½", dec 1 st each side on last row. Work 1¼" more. Bind off. With RS facing, work in pat across rem 8 sts. Work approx ½" in k2, p2 rib. Work another ½" in seed st, dec 1 st at beg of last RS row. Work another 1½" in seed st. Bind off.

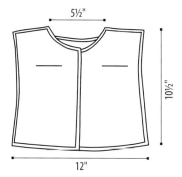

Size 1-2 yrs.

Finished measurements Chest 24". Length 10 ½".

Yarns 1 ball sport weight yarn (each 1¾oz/50g, approx 136yd/125m) each in Light Blue, Medium Blue, Navy, Yellow, Brown, Red and Multi.

Needles One pair each sizes 1 and 5 (2.25 and 3.75mm) needles, *or size to obtain gauge*. Size 5 (3.75mm) circular needle, 24"/60cm, and double-pointed needles (dpn).

Extras Stitch holders and markers. One 1" bear button. Odd bits of yarn for stuffing. Size B/1 (2mm) crochet hook.

Gauge 22 sts and 30 rows to 4" (10cm) over St st using size 5 (3.75mm) needles.

Seed st arm With yellow, cast on 4 sts. Beg on row 24 of Chart for Back, work in seed st and shape piece using arm outline as guide. With brown, work 1 row sc evenly around piece. Tack arm at lower and upper edges into position, leaving sides open.

Right and Left Fronts

Pocket linings (make 2) With light blue, cast on 20 sts. Work 2" in St st. Place sts on hold.

Pocket pieces (make 2) With red, cast on 19 sts. K 4 rows. **Rows 1 and 3** P4, k3, p5, k3, p4. **Rows 2 and 4** K4, p3, k5, p3, k4. **Rows 5 and 7** [K3, p5] twice, k3. **Rows 6 and 8** [P3, k5] twice, p3. Rep rows 1-8 twice more, dec 1 st each side on last 3 rows. Bind off all sts.

Fronts With navy, cast on 32 sts. [P 1 row, k 1 row] twice. Work Chart for Right or Left Front, inserting pocket lining as foll: On row 58, p6, place next 20 sts on hold, then p across 20 sts of pocket lining, p to end. Shape neck as indicated. Bind off all sts.

Pocket edgings With WS facing and light blue, k across 20 sts on hold. K 2 rows, binding off on 2nd row. Tack edgings to fronts. Sew pocket linings in place. Sew pocket pieces onto fronts.

Finishing

Block pieces. Sew shoulder seams. Using photo and chart as guide, sew tree to back, leaving opening at side of trunk, and at top between 2 shorter branches. Sew I-cord, leaving approx 2" open right after branch.

Front and side edgings

With RS facing, circular needle and navy, beg at right front cast-on row and pick up and k to 1¼" before neck shaping, cast-on 5 sts, leave a ¾" space for buttonhole, then cont to pick up along front edge, around neck and to left front edge cast-on row. Beg with a k row, work 6 rows in rev St st. Bind off loosely. Turn edge and tack to WS. In same way, pick up sts evenly along each side and work edging.

I-cord trim

With dpn and navy, work 3-st I-cord to fit along each shoulder, twisting to form a play loop. Sew along shoulder seams. Work four 6" I-cord strips and sew to sides for ties.

MINI BEARS

Separate yarn into 3 strands. Work with 2 strands held tog and save 3rd strand for stuffing. Use colors as desired to work body parts.

Legs and Body

With smaller needles, cast on 13 st. K 2 rows. [K1 row, p1

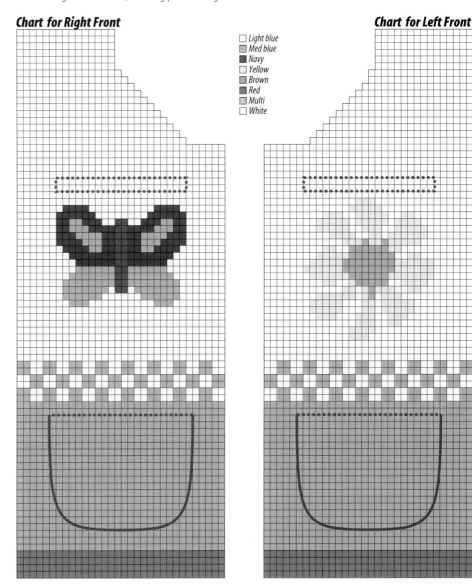

Chart for Right Front

Chart for Left Front

☐ Light blue
▨ Med blue
■ Navy
☐ Yellow
▨ Brown
■ Red
▨ Multi
☐ White

row] 4 times. Place sts on hold. Make 2nd leg. Do not cut yarn. K across 13 sts, then k 13 sts of first leg—26 sts. Work 13 rows more in St st for body.

Shape neck

Next row (RS) *K1, k2tog; rep from* across, end k2—18 sts. **Next row** *P1, p2tog; rep from* across—12 sts.

Shape head

Next row (RS) K1, [k1, M1] 10 times, k1—22 sts. Work 8 rows in St st. **Next row** P6, place marker (pm), p10, pm, p6. **Next row** Knit across and k2tog before and after each marker. **Next row** P across and p2tog before and after each marker. **Next row** K across and k2tog before first and after 2nd marker. Bind off purlwise.

Stuffing piece lightly as you sew, fold legs to inside and sew seams. Sew back and head seam.

Arms (make 2)

Cast on 12 sts. K 2 rows. Work 8 rows in St st. Bind off all sts. Fold in half, sew seam and stuff lightly. Sew to bear.

Ears

Pick up and k approx 8 sts along top half of head. Dec 1 st each side every row and p 1 row, then k 1 row. Bind off rem sts.

With navy, embroider eyes, nose and mouth on bear's face. Tie length of red yarn around neck in bow.

Chart for Back

INTERMEDIATE

Back

With MC, cast on 48 (54, 60, 66) sts with MC. Join CC and work as foll: **Row 1** (WS) *P3 MC, p3 CC; rep from* across. **Row 2** K1 MC, *k3 CC, k3 MC; rep from*, end k2 MC. **Row 3** P1 MC, *p3 CC, p3 MC; rep from* across, end p2 MC. **Row 4** *K3 MC, k3 CC; rep from* across. **Row 5** P2 CC, *p3 MC, p3 CC; rep from* across, end p1 CC. **Row 6** K2 CC, *k3 MC, k3 CC; rep from* across, end k1 CC. Rep rows 1-6 for diagonal pat, moving 3-st diagonal stripes over 1 st on every row. When piece measures 12 (13, 14, 15)" from beg, bind off all sts with MC.

Front

Work as for back until piece measures 9 (10, 11, 12)" from beg, end with a WS row.

Shape neck

Next row (RS) Cont pat, k21 (23, 25, 28), join 2nd ball of yarn and bind off 6 (8, 10, 10) sts, k to end. Working both sides at same time, bind off 2 sts from each neck edge once. Dec 1 st at each neck edge every row 5 times. Work even on rem 14 (16, 18, 21) sts each side until piece measures same as back to shoulder. Bind off all sts.

Sleeves

Cast on 28 (28, 30, 30) sts with MC. Work 9 rows in k1, p1 rib. Change to CC. Cont in St st, AT SAME TIME, inc 1 st each side every 4th row 9 (11, 8, 10) times, every 6th row 0 (0, 2, 3) times—46 (50, 50, 56) sts. Work even until piece measures 11 (12, 13, 15)" from beg. Bind off all sts.

Finishing

Block pieces. Sew shoulder seams.

Neck

With RS facing, circular needle and MC, beg at right shoulder and pick up and k 54 (58, 62, 62) sts evenly around neck.

Place marker, join and work 2½ " in k1, p1 rib. Bind off loosely in rib. Fold neckband and tack to WS. Place markers 6½ (7, 7, 8)" down from shoulders on front and back. Sew top of sleeves between markers. Sew side and sleeve seams.

Fringe

Cut 2 lengths of yarn, each 7" long. Holding strands tog, fold in half and with a crochet hook, pull through a cast-on st of the same color. Pull ends of yarn through loop. In same way, make MC and CC fringe and attach around lower edge. Trim fringe.

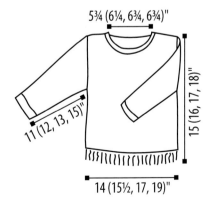

5¾ (6¼, 6¾, 6¾)"

15 (16, 17, 18)"

11 (12, 13, 15)"

14 (15½, 17, 19)"

I am an Australian living in Chicago and have been knitting since I was 5. I used to take my knitting to school to knit during recess. Since moving to America, I have received an Associate in Fashion Design at Harper College. I concentrated on children's clothes, winning first place in the 1995 Fashion Group Foundation Children's Wear contest. I like to design clothes that are fun because that's what kids' clothes should be. As my kids get older they like more subtle colors but I keep pushing for the brights. When knitting for kids, make sure you use good quality, washable wools and use plenty of bright colors. You'll have something that's easy to care for, keeps the child warm and still looks great after being washed. Kids are full of light and energy and this should be reflected in the bright clothes they wear. A garment does not have to have a lot of detail as long as it has bright colors.

Sizes 4 (6, 8, 10). Shown in size 6.

Measurements Chest 28 (31, 34, 38)". Length (including 3" fringe) 15 (16, 17, 18)".

Yarn 4 (5, 6, 7) balls in chunky weight yarn (each 1¾oz/50g, approx 68yd/62m) each in Fuchsia multi (MC) and White multi (CC).

Needles One pair size 10 (6mm) needles, *or size to obtain gauge*. Size 9 (5.5mm) circular needle, 16"/40cm.

Extras Stitch holders and markers. Size D/3 (3mm) crochet hook.

Gauge 14 sts and 18 rows to 4" (10cm) in St st using size 10 (6mm) needles and MC.

Royal Velvet Cardigan

ADVANCED BEGINNER

EDITOR'S NOTE Body is knitted in one piece to the underarm, then divided for back and fronts.

Body

With smaller needles, cast on 216 (232, 244) sts. K 4 (4, 6) rows. Change to larger needles. Beg with a k row, work in St st (k on RS, p on WS) until piece measures 7 (8, 10)" from beg, end with a RS row.

Next (dec) row (WS) **Size 1** *P1, p2tog; rep from* across—144 sts. **Size 2** P2, *[p1, p2tog] 5 times, p2 p2tog; rep from* across, end p2—160 sts. **Size 4** P3, *p1, p2tog, p2 p2tog; rep from* across, end p3—176 sts.

For all sizes K 1 row on RS, then k 1 row on WS for first garter ridge. Beg with a k row, work 4 rows in St st.

Divide for underarms and work 2nd garter ridge: Next row (WS) K36 (40, 44) sts (left front) and place sts on hold; k72 (80, 88) sts (back) and place sts on hold; k to end (right front). Turn.

Right Front

Cont on 36 (40, 44) sts of right front only. **Establish pat: Rib row 1** (RS) P1, *k1, p4; rep from* 6 (6, 7) times more, k0 (1, 1), p0 (3, 2). **Rib row 2** (WS) K0 (3, 2), p0 (1, 1), *k4, p1; rep from* 6 (6, 7) times more, end k1. Rep rib rows 1-2 until piece measures 4 (4½, 5)" from dividing row, end with rib row 2.

Shape neck

Next row (RS) Bind off 4 (5, 6) sts, cont rib pat to end. **Next row** (WS) Cont rib pat on rem sts. Rep last 2 rows twice more. Work 3 rows even on rem 24 (25, 26) sts. Bind off in pat.

Left Front

Slip 36 (40, 44) sts of left front onto needle, ready to work a RS row. **Establish pat: Rib row 1** (RS) P0 (3, 2), k0 (1, 1), *p4, k1; rep from* 6 (6, 7) times more, end p1. **Rib row 2** (WS) K1, *p1, k4; rep from* 6 (6, 7) times more, p0 (1, 1), k0 (3, 2). Rep rib rows 1-2 until piece measures same as right front to neck, end with rib row 1. Shape neck by binding off at beg of WS rows. Complete as for right front.

Back

Slip 72 (80, 88) sts of back onto needle, ready to work a RS row. **Establish pat: Rib row 1** (RS) P3 (2, 1), *k1, p4; rep from* 12 (14, 16) times, k1, p3 (2, 1). **Rib row 2** (WS) K3 (2, 1), p1, *k4, p1; rep from* 12 (14, 16) times, k3 (2, 1). Rep rib rows 1-2 until piece measures same as fronts to shoulder. Bind off all sts.

Sleeves

With smaller needles, cast on 38 (42, 44) sts. Work 1½" in k1, p1 rib. Change to larger needles. K 2 rows. Cont in St st, AT SAME TIME, inc 1 st each side (working incs into St st) every 4th row 11 (12, 14) times—60 (66, 72) sts. Work even until piece measures 10 (11, 12)" from beg, end with a WS row. K 2 rows. Bind off all sts.

Finishing

Block pieces lightly. Sew shoulder seams. Set in sleeves. Sew sleeve seams. Cut ribbon (making sure it begins and ends alike) to fit around entire garment at underarm. Sew ribbon to garment in St st section between garter ridges at underarm. OR apply fabric glue to ribbon and apply in St st section between garter ridges. Let dry overnight.

Using photo as guide, place 5 (6, 7) markers for buttonholes on right front below ribbon and 4 (4, 5) markers above ribbon.

Edging With RS facing and crochet hook, join yarn to lower right front edge and work 1 row sc evenly around both fronts and neck edge, working button loops at markers by ch 5, skip 2 sts, then cont sc.

Optional: Paint center 'petals' of buttons to match flower ribbons. Sew buttons on.

Optional: With tapestry needle, weave green yarn through garter st loops around sleeve cuffs.

Sizes 1 (2, 4) yrs. Shown in size 2.

Finished measurements Chest (buttoned) 26 (29, 32)". Length 13 (14½, 17)".

Yarns 4 (5, 6) balls sport weight chenille (each 1¾oz/50g, approx 136yd/125m) in Denim blue.

Needles One pair each sizes 4 and 5 (3.5 and 3.75mm) needles, *or size to obtain gauge.*

Extras Stitch holders and markers. Size D/3 (3mm) crochet hook. 9 (10, 12) white flower buttons, each ⅝" (15mm). Approx 27 (31, 33)" floral ribbon, ⅝" wide. Fabric glue. Optional: Small amount green yarn.

Gauge 22 sts and 24 rows to 4" (10cm) over St st using size 5 (3.75mm) needles.

I work as a research technician in a genetic research laboratory. It's exciting work but I needed something creative to balance this. Knitting proved to be the perfect outlet for my creative energies and I now have a part-time knitting/design business.
I love to develop new ideas, play with color and texture, and work out technical details. This garment was designed to be an easy pattern for beginners, with a strong sense of style from color and add-on design elements. The ribbon, found in a specialty store, was actually the starting point for the pattern. White buttons were painted to complete the look.

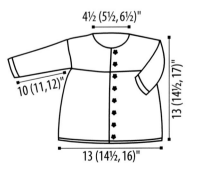

4½ (5½, 6½)"

10 (11,12)"

13 (14½, 17)"

13 (14½, 16)"

Baa, baa, black sheep...

KIDS CONTEST

Baa, baa, black sheep,

Have you any wool?

Yes, sir, yes, sir,

Three bags full.

One for my master,

One for my dame,

And one for the little boy

Who lives in the lane.

Accessories

Knit Hat

MELISSA ADAMS
REDMOND, WASHINGTON

INTERMEDIATE

Knitting for children can be a quick way to test new design ideas and shapes. I really enjoy playing with patterns, colors and embellished edges and trims, as in these two variations of the same hat.

EDITOR'S NOTE The same set of instructions apply for Versions A and B. Only the colors and crown instructions change. Use the colors as noted in 'Yarns.' Change to double-pointed needles (dpn) when necessary.

Brim

With MC and circular needle, cast on 128 (134, 140) sts. Place marker and join, being careful not to twist sts. **Rnds 1-4** Work in k1, p1 rib. **Rnd 5** K 1 rnd and inc 4 (6, 6) sts evenly around—132 (140, 146) sts. **Rnds 6-11** With A, k 6 rnds. **Rnd 12 (tuck rnd)** With A and tip of left needle, pick up purl bump of first st from first rnd of A, then knit it tog with next st on left needle, *k1; skip next st from first rnd and pick up purl bump after skipped st, then knit it tog with next st on needle; rep from* around, knitting tog every other st from first rnd. **Rnds 13-18** With MC, knit and inc 1 (0, 1) st in rnd 18—133 (140, 147) sts. **Rnds19-39** With MC and B, work 21 rnds of chart, working 7-st rep around. **Rnds 40-45** With MC, knit and dec 1 (0, 1) st in rnd 45—132 (140, 146) sts. **Rnds 46-49** With A, knit. **Rnd 50** With A, *k2tog, yo; rep from* around. **Rnds 51-54** With A, knit. **Rnd 55** Rep rnd 12 (tuck rnd).

Crown: Version A (Round)

Rnd 1 With MC, k and inc 1 (0, 1) st—133 (140, 147) sts. **Rnd 2** With MC, *k5, k2tog; rep from* around—114 (120, 126) sts. **Rnds 3, 5, 6, 8 and 9** With MC, knit. **Rnd 4** With MC, *k5, k2tog; rep from* around, end k2 (1, 0)—98 (103, 108) sts. **Rnd 7** With MC, *k4, k2tog; rep from* around, end k2 (1, 0)—82 (86, 90) sts. **Rnd 10** With MC, *k4, k2tog; rep from* around, end k2 (2, 6), k2tog size S—68 (72, 76) sts. **Rnd 11** *K1 MC, k1 C; rep from* around. **Rnds 12 and 14** With C, knit. **Rnd 13** With C, purl. **Rnd 15** *K1 C, k1 MC; rep from* around. **Rnds 16 and 17** With MC, knit. **Rnd 18** With MC, *k3, k2tog; rep from* around, end k1 (2, 1), k2tog Size S—54 (58,61) sts. **Rnds 19, 21, 22, 24 and 25** With MC, knit. **Rnd 20** With MC, *k2, k2tog; rep from* around, end k0 (2, 1), k2tog size S—40 (44, 46) sts. **Rnd 23** With MC, *k2, k2tog; rep from* around, end k2tog size L—30 (33, 34) sts. **Rnd 26** With MC, *k2, k2tog; rep from* around, end k0 (1, 0), k2tog sizes S and L—22 (25, 25) sts. **Rnd 27** With B, *p1, p2tog; rep from*, end p1—15 (17, 17) sts. **Rnd 28** With B, knit. **Rnd 29** With B, *k1, k2tog; rep from* around, end k0 (2, 2)—10 (12, 12) sts. **Rnd 30** With B, k2tog around—5 (6, 6) sts. Cut yarn, leaving a 6" tail. Pull tail through rem sts, tighten and fasten off.

Crown: Version B (Square)

Rnd 1 With MC, k and inc 0 (0, 2) sts—132 (140, 148) sts. **Rnd 2** With MC, k15 (16, 17), S2KP2, *k30 (32, 34), S2KP2; rep from* twice, k15 (16, 17). **Rnd 3** With MC, k14 (15, 16), S2KP2, *k28 (30, 32), S2KP2; rep from* twice, k14 (15, 16). **Rnd 4** With MC, k13 (14, 15), S2KP2, *k26 (28, 30), S2KP2; rep from* twice, k13 (14, 15). Cont in same way, working S2KP2 at corners and working 2 sts less between decs to 68 (68, 76) sts. **Ridge Rnd 1** *K1 MC, k1 C; rep from* around. **Rnds 2 and 4** With C, k working SK2P2 at corners. **Rnd 3** With C, purl. **Rnd 5** *K1 C, k1 MC; rep from* around. **For all sizes:** K with MC, working S2KP2 at corners, to 20 sts. **Next rnd** With B, *p2, p2tog; rep from* around. Work rnds 28-30 as for size S, Version A. Complete as for Version A.

Finishing

Block lightly, being sure to press top of hat flat.

Tassel Using photo as guide, make tassel with B and wrap with A. Sew to top of hat.

Sizes S (M, L). Shown in size Medium.

Finished measurements Circumference approx 18 (19, 20)."

Yarns **Version A** 1 ball sport weight yarn (each 1¾oz/50g, 136yd/124m) each in Moss green (MC) and Gold (B). Small amount in Eggplant (A) and Medium gray (C). **Version B** 1 ball each Eggplant (MC) and Gold (B). Small amount in Gray (A) and Moss green (C).

Needles Size 3 (3.25mm) circular needle, 16"/40cm long, *or size to obtain gauge*. Size 3 (3.25mm) double pointed needles (dpn).

Extras Stitch markers.

Gauge 29 sts and 40 rows to 4" (10cm) over Chart pat using size 3 (3.25mm) dpn.

Chart

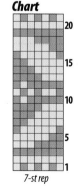

7-st rep

■ Moss Green/Eggplant
□ Gold

BEGINNER

EDITOR'S NOTE The hat is knit, felted in hot water until it fits, then dyed with Kool Aid. For best results, use an animal fiber such as 100% wool that has not been treated to be a super-wash yarn. After making one hat and seeing how it felts, try casting on more sts for a slightly larger hat or fewer sts for a smaller hat.

Hat

Cast on 70 sts. Place marker and join, being careful not to twist sts. Work even until piece measures 15" from beg. **Dec rnd 1** *K5, k2tog; rep from* around—60 sts. K 2 rnds. **Dec rnd 2** *K2, k2tog; rep from* around—45 sts. K 10 rnds. Bind off all sts.

Gather top: Cut a 50" strand of yarn and thread through a tapestry needle. Working with yarn double, sew in and out around the last rnd of decs (dec rnd 2), leaving about 8" of yarn. Pull the yarn ends tight and gather the top of the hat closed. Wrap the 2 ends of yarn very tightly around the gathers and tie them into a knot. Secure the ends and fasten off.

Magic step #1 - Shrink to fit

Fill a dish pan half full of hot water. Add a tiny drop of liquid dish soap, then put the hat into the pan. Using both hands, squeeze the water through the hat, being sure to squeeze water through all parts. Keep squeezing for about 10 minutes. Notice that the yarn is beginning to feel tighter as it's shrinking. Squeeze for another 10 minutes and then squeeze out as much water as you can. Fold up the bottom of the hat and try it on or measure it flat across the brim. An 8" wide brim will yield a small hat. Aim for 9" wide for a medium and 10" wide for a large kid's hat. If still too big, add some more hot water and keep on squeezing. If you get tired, leave the hat in the water and take a break. Continue to squeeze the hat in hot water until it is the right size. Rinse the hat in cold water, then squeeze out all the excess, being careful not to pull or stretch your hat out of shape. Fold up the brim and set the hat on a towel. Let it dry overnight.

Magic step #2 - Dye the hat

Put 4 cups of very hot water in a big, deep pot (a canning kettle works well). Open 2 packets of Kool Aid mix, pour in the pot and stir to dissolve. Add ½ cup of vinegar. Take your hat and moisten it with water, then set it into the kettle with the Kool Aid. Don't push it all the way under the water; just let it 'stand' there. Every 5 minutes, add 4 more cups of very hot water to the kettle. Continue to do this until the water comes as high up to the top of the hat as you want. As you add water, the dye color will be lighter and lighter. Leave the hat sitting in the dye bath until the water is cool. Rinse your hat in cool water and squeeze out the excess water. Let it dry overnight as before.

Magic step #3 - The crowning touches

Now that the hat is felted and dyed, you can add your own special touches. Here are some possibilities:
- take a pair of very sharp scissors and cut part way down the top knot to make a fringe (as shown in photo).
- use the scissors to cut a wavy or jagged edge on the brim.
- sew buttons or bells along the edge of the brim or on the crown of the hat.
- embroider designs on your hat.

As a reference librarian, I get lots of mental stimulation but then appreciate going home to the cedars, alders, cats, wild birds, gardens, and knitting— heaven! Because I enjoy the rhythm and quieting nature of knitting, I'm drawn to projects with simple lines and a straightforward approach. Here is a multi-stage project that gives surprising results with each step, yet it uses no exotic tools or equipment and is forgiving to the likely errors of a beginning knitter. And, on top of all this, the felting process can almost guarantee a hat that will fit.

Sizes S, M or L.

Yarns Approx 4 oz worsted weight wool in any light color.

Needles Size 10½ (6.5mm) circular needle, 16"/40cm long, *or size to obtain gauge.*

Extras 2 packages of Unsweetened Kool Aid. ½ cup vinegar. Large pot or canning kettle. Rubber gloves. Tapestry needle.

Gauge 16 sts and 24 rows to 4" (10cm) over St st using size 10½ (6.5mm) needle.

Hansel and Gretel

EXPERIENCED

I have loved fairy tales all of my life. The story of Hansel and Gretel and their struggle to outsmart the mean old witch in the gingerbread house is a classic. Hansel and Gretel are devoted brother and sister. Most of the time, clever Hansel can solve the problems that befall them. But, when things get out of hand and he is caged by the witch, all seems lost. Until dear, sweet Gretel rises to the occasion and becomes the heroine—then the children get their just deserts! That is the best part of the story for this sweet-toothed fairy tale fancier.

Finished measurements Each approx 5½" long

Yarns For Hansel, Gretel and the Witch oddments of fingering weight yarns in Black (A), Fleshtone (B), Green (C), Cream (D) and Gray (E). Bouclé yarn for hair in Cream (F) and Gray (G).

Needles 2 sets of size 0 (2mm) double pointed needles (dpn), *or size to obtain gauge.*

Extras Two ¼"and one ⅜" buttons; 4 red sequins for cheeks. Embroidery floss for eyes, mouth and eyebrows. Stuffing. Tapestry needle. Stitch markers and holders.

Gauge 36 sts and 54 rows to 4" (10cm) over St st using size 0 (2mm) dpn.

HANSEL

**Legs (make 2)

With dpn and A, leave a tail, cast on 8 sts and divide evenly over 3 dpn. Place marker and join, being careful not to twist sts. **Rnd 1** Knit. **Rnd 2** *K1, M1; rep from* around—16 sts. **Rnds 3-6** Knit. **Rnd 7** K1, *k1, k2tog; rep from* around—11 sts. **Rnd 8** Knit. **Rnds 9-18** With B, knit. **Rnd 19** With C, knit. **Rnd 20** With C, purl. **Rnds 21-26** With C, knit. Leave sts on hold.

Join legs With C, graft first 3 sts of legs tog to form crotch—16 sts. **Rnd 27** With C, k around rem sts from both legs and pick up 1 st at front and back of crotch (placing marker at beg of rnd)—18 sts.**

Shorts With C, k 8 rnds, then p 2 rnds for waistband. Bind off all sts. Weave tail through cast-on sts of each foot, tighten and fasten off.

Bib With RS facing and C, pick up and k the 6 center front sts. P the first and last st every row, work 5 rows in St st, then work 2 rows in rev St st. Bind off all sts.

Shirt With RS facing and D, pick up and k 18 sts along inside of waistband and divide evenly over 3 dpn. Place marker, join and k 9 rnds. Leave sts on hold.

***(*) Arms (make 2)

With dpn and B, leave a tail, cast on 11 sts and divide over 3 dpn. Place marker and join, being careful not to twist sts. **Rnds 1-7** Knit. **Rnd 8** With D, knit. **Rnd 9** With D, purl. **Rnds 10-26** With D, knit. Graft 3 sts of left arm tog with 3 sts of left body for underarm. Keeping these underarm sts in line with outside of legs, k to other underarm and rep for right side. Divide sts over 3 dpn, placing marker between 4th and 5th st on right arm—28 sts. Weave tail through cast-on sts at beg of each arm, tighten and fasten off. Stuff legs, body and arms. K 2 rnds over all sts, end at marker.

Shape neck Rnd 1 With D, k2, [S2KP2, k4] 3 times, S2KP2, k2—20 sts. **Rnds 2, 4 and 6** With D, knit. **Rnd 3** With D, k1, [S2KP2, K2] 3 times, S2KP, k1—12 sts. **Rnd 5** With D, k1, [k2tog] twice, k1, [S2KP2] twice—6 sts. **Rnd 7** With B, knit. **Rnd 8** With B, [k1, M1] 6 times—12 sts. **Rnd 9** With B, knit. (*) **Rnd 10** With B, [k2, M1] 6 times—18 sts. **Rnds 11-16** With B, k 6 rnds. Cut yarn, leaving an 8" tail. Stuff head and neck. Pull yarn through 18 sts, tighten and fasten off.***

Finishing

Straps (make 2)

With C, cast on 3 sts and k every row for approx 2". Crossing straps at back, sew to waistband, then sew to bib at front, topping with ¼" buttons. Using photo as guide, embroider face, then attach sequins as cheeks. Stitch bouclé yarn (F) onto head for hair.

GRETEL

Work as for Hansel from** to **, using D instead of C to start underwear.

Underwear K 8 rnds. Place all sts on hold.

Skirt With E, cast on 54 sts and divide evenly over 3 dpn. Place marker and join, being careful not to twist sts. **Rnds 1 and 3** Purl. **Rnd 2** Knit. **Rnds 4-11** Knit. **Rnd 12** *K1, k2tog; rep from* around—36 sts. **Rnds 13-15** Knit. **Rnd 16** *K1, k2tog; rep from* around—24 sts. **Rnds 17-18** Knit. **Rnd 19** *K2, k2tog; rep from* around—18 sts. **Rnd 20** Knit.

Attach skirt to body Keeping skirt sts on needle, slip skirt over body and k 1 st of each piece tog to end of rnd—18 sts. K 7 rnds.

Work as for Hansel from*** to ***, using E instead of D.

Finishing

Apron

With D, cast on 15 sts. **Rows 1-11** Beg with a p row, work in St st. **Rows 12-17** Knit. Bind off all sts. With RS facing and D, pick up and k 2 sts at top of apron edge. Make a 2-st I-cord for apron string, approx 3½" long. Fasten off. Rep for other apron string. Tie around waist. Using photo as guide, embroider face and attach sequins as cheeks. Stitch bouclé yarn F onto head for hair, leaving 3 longer strands on each side of face. Braid the 3 strands tog and fasten off. With black embroidery floss, form dress tie on chest.

WITCH

Legs (make 2)

With dpn and A, cast on 8 sts and divide evenly over 3 dpn. Place marker and join, being careful not to twist sts. **Rnd 1** Knit. **Rnd 2** *K1, M1; rep from* around—16 sts. **Rnds 3-6** Knit. **Rnd 7** K1, *k1, k2tog; rep from* around—11 sts. **Rnd 8** Knit. **Rnds 9-10** With E, knit. **Rnds 11-12** With C, knit. **Rnds 13-24** Rep rnds 9-12. Leave sts on hold.

Join legs Graft first 3 sts of legs tog to form crotch—16 sts. **Rnd 25** With E, k around rem sts from both legs and pick up 1 st at front and back of crotch (place marker at beg of rnd)—18 sts. **Rnd 26** With E, knit. **Rnds 27-28** With C, knit. **Rnds 29-30** With E, knit. **Rnds 31-34** Rep rnds 27-30. Leave all sts on hold.

Skirt With A, cast on 54 sts and divide evenly over 3 dpn. Place marker and join, being careful not to twist sts.

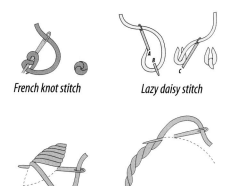

French knot stitch

Lazy daisy stitch

Satin stitch

Outline stitch

Twisted cord

1. Cut strands 6 times the length of cord needed. Fold in half and knot the cut ends together.

2. With knotted end in left hand and right index finger in folded end, twist clockwise until cord is tightly twisted.

3. Fold cord in half and smooth as it twists on itself; knot.

Finished measurement approx 7" x 7" long.

Yarns For gingerbread house purse 2 balls worsted weight yarn (each 1¾oz/50g, 110yd/100m) in Brown (MC); oddments in White (A), Red (B) and Green (C). White lurex (D) in fingering weight yarn. Gold embroidery floss.

Needles Sizes 0 and 5 (2 and 3.75mm) needles, *or size to obtain gauge*. Size C/2 (2.5mm) crochet hook.

Extras Three ⅝" buttons.One gold ¾" button. Assorted beads and buttons (some in crystal iridescent) for decoration. Beading needle. Sewing thread and needle.

Gauge 19 sts and 28 rows to 4" (10cm) over St st using size 5 (3.75mm) needles.

Rnds 1 and 3 Purl. **Rnd 2** Knit. **Rnds 4-14** Knit. **Rnd 15** *K1, k2tog; rep from* around—36 sts. **Rnds 16-19** Knit. **Rnd 20** *K1, k2tog; rep from* around—24 sts. **Rnds 21-22** Knit. **Rnd 23** *K2, k2tog; rep from* around—18 sts. **Rnd 24** Knit. Attach skirt to body as for Gretel—18 sts. **Rnds 25-31** Knit. Work arms and shape neck as for Hansel from (*) to (*), using A instead of D. **Next rnd** *[K1, M1] twice, k1; rep from* around—20 sts. K 6 rnds. Cut yarn, leaving an 8" tail. Stuff head and neck. Pull yarn through all sts, tighten and fasten off.

Finishing

Shawl With E, cast on 35 sts. K 2 rows. Cont in garter st and shape as foll: *Next row K1, ssk, k to last 3 sts, k2tog, k1—33 sts. K 1 row. Rep from* until 3 sts rem, end S2KP2. Fasten off.

Fringe Cut approx 1½" long strands of E. Using photo as guide, fold each in half and attach to shaped edges of shawl. Trim evenly. Wrap shawl around Witch's neck and secure with ¾" button.

Embroider face. Stitch bouclé yarn G onto head for hair leaving longer strands at back. Make ponytail at back by tying strands tog with A.

GINGERBREAD HOUSE PURSE

With size 5 (3.75mm) needles and A, cast on 33 sts. **Row 1** Knit. **Row 2** Purl. **Row 3** With MC, k1, *sl 1 with yarn in back (wyib), k5; rep from* 4 times more, sl 1 wyib, k1. **Rows 4 and 6** With MC, p1, *sl 1 with yarn in front (wyif), p5; rep from* 4 times more, sl 1 wyif, p1. **Row 5** (buttonhole row) With MC, k1, *sl 1 wyib, k2, yo, k2tog, k1, sl 1 wyib, k5; rep from* once more, sl 1 wyib, k2, yo, k2tog, k1, sl 1 wyib, k1. **Rows 7 and 8** With A, knit. **Rows 9 and 11** With MC, k4, *sl 1 wyib, k5; rep from* 3 times more, sl 1 wyib, k4. **Rows 10 and 12** With MC, p4, *sl 1 wyif, p5; rep from* 3 times more, sl 1 wyif, p4. **Rows 13 and 14** With A, knit. Rep rows 3-14 once more, omitting buttonholes (yo, k2tog).

With MC, work 53 rows in St st. **Next row** (WS) Knit to form turning ridge.

Work chart Work rows 1-31 of chart, using separate strands of yarn for each color. Twist colors on wrong side to prevent holes. **Next row** (WS) With MC, k1, *p1, k1; rep from* to end. Rep last row 4 times more. Bind off in pat.

Windows (make 2)

With size 0 (2mm) needles and D, cast on 7 sts. Work 15 rows in St st. Bind off purlwise.

Finishing

Using photo as guide, sew windows in place. Use beads and embroidery to embellish and decorate purse as desired. Sew or crochet side seams.

With RS facing, crochet hook and A, sc down side of roof, work picot along cast on edge as foll: 1 sc, *ch 3, 3 sc ; rep from* along edge; end ch 3, 1 sc. Work sc evenly along other side of roof. Sew buttons on.

Cord (make 2)

Cut 3 strands of MC and make a twisted cord approx 17" long. Attach to outer roof edges, knot ends together.

Chart

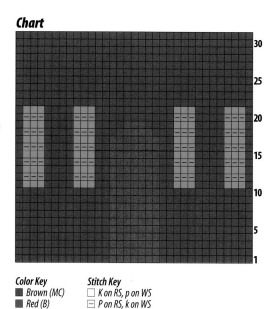

Color Key
■ Brown (MC)
■ Red (B)
■ Green (C)

Stitch Key
☐ K on RS, p on WS
⊟ P on RS, k on WS

ADVANCED BEGINNER

Make 1 (M1) Insert left needle from front to back under horizontal strand between st just knitted and next st. K into back of strand to make new st.

RIGHT HAND

**With MC, cast on 32 sts. Work 14 rows in k1, p1 rib. Beg with a k row, work 8 rows in St st.

Thumb gusset

Row 1 (RS) K16, M1, k1, M1, k15—34 sts. **Rows 2, 4, 6, 8, 10 and 12** Purl. **Row 3** K16, M1, k3, M1, k15—36 sts. **Row 5** K16, M1, k5, M1, k15—38 sts. **Row 7** K16, M1, k7, M1, k15—40 sts. **Row 9** K16, M1, k9, M1, k15—42 sts. **Row 11** K16, M1, k11, M1, k15—44 sts.

Thumb

Row 1 K30 and place rem sts on hold. Turn. **Row 2** P14 and place rem sts on hold. Turn. **Rows 3, 5 and 7** Knit. **Rows 4, 6 and 8** Purl. Work rows 9-13 with A. **Row 9** Knit. **Row 10** Purl. **Row 11** K2tog across—7 sts. **Row 12** Purl. **Row 13** [K2tog] 3 times, k1—4 sts. Cut yarn, leaving a 7" tail. Pull tail through rem sts, tighten and fasten off. Sew thumb seam.

Palm

Row 1 With RS facing (thumb pointing forward) and MC, pick up and k 2 sts along base of thumb, then k14 sts on hold. **Row 2** P16, then p next 16 sts on hold—32 sts. **Rows 3, 5, 7, 9** Knit. **Rows 4, 6, 8, 10** Purl. Cut yarn, leaving a 7" tail. **Row 11** Place first 4 sts on hold. With B, M1, k24, M1. Place last 4 sts on hold—26 sts. Turn. **Row 12** (WS) Purl 26.** **Row 13** K13 MC, k13 A. **Row 14** P13 A, p13 MC. **Rows 15-24** Rep last 2 rows. **Row 25** With MC, [k2tog] 6 times, k1; with A, [k2tog] 6 times, k1—14 sts. **Row 26** With A, [p2tog] 3 times, p1; with MC, [p2tog] 3 times, p1. With MC, bind off rem

8 sts. Cut yarn, leaving a 6" tail. Sew seam up to sts on hold.

Baby finger

Row 1 With RS facing and MC, k 4 sts on hold, pick up and k2 sts from base of finger section, then k next 4 sts on hold—10 sts. **Rows 2, 4, 6 and 8** Purl. **Rows 3, 5 and 7** Knit. **Rows 9 and 10** With A, k 1 row, then p 1 row. **Row 11** With A, [k2tog] 5 times—5 sts. Cut yarn, leaving a 6" tail. Pull tail through rem sts, tighten and fasten off. Sew baby finger seam and side seam.

LEFT HAND

Work as for Right Hand from ** to **. Reverse face colors on palm as foll: **Row 13** K13A, k13 MC. Complete as for right hand.

Finishing

Using photo as guide, embroider hair and faces.

I work part time, do a bit of volunteer work at several churches, and love to knit for my granddaughter, Courtney. She is the one who started me knitting—she wanted doll clothes so I taught myself by making a little scarf and blankie for her dolls, then sweaters, booties and mittens for all her little 'friends.' Each year Courtney purges her toy box, and each year I still see the doll/bear clothes in the box. One day we were in a gift shop and they had bears with knit sweaters and accessories. I said I'd get some for her and she said "No grandma, my little friends only want to wear what you made for them, they feel more special." To love someone is to knit for them. Oh, do you know the containers that the long fireplace matches come in? They are great for small projects. Needles and a ball of yarn fit in nicely. I also use them for just the needles— I always had needles poking out of my bag. No more!

Sizes To fit a child between 3 and 5 yrs.

Yarns 1 ball sport weight yarn (each 1¾oz/50g, approx 136yd/124m) in Dark pink (MC). Small amounts of Light pink (A) and White (B).

Needles One pair size 5 (3.75mm) needles, *or size to obtain gauge.*

Extras Embroidery thread for faces and hair. 2 sequins for eyes. Stitch holder.

Gauge 22 sts and 32 rows to 4" (10cm) over St st using size 5 (3.75mm) needles.

Puppets Galore!

INTERMEDIATE

Sizes To fit a child between 5 and 10 yrs, depending on the yarn used.

Measurements Wrist approx 7" for smaller mittens, 8" for larger mittens.

Yarns 1 ball of sport or worsted weight yarn (each 1¾oz/50g) in main color (MC) and small amounts of all other colors.

Dragon Dark green (MC), Olive green (A), Bright green (B), Red (C).

Whale Gray (MC), Red (A), Blue (B).

Kitten White (MC), Pink (A), Light blue (B). Small amount white felt. White sewing yarn and sewing needle.

Puppy Gold (MC), Beige (A), Light brown (B), Black (C).

Pony Natural (MC), Light brown (A), Gold (B), Brown (C).

Goldfish Bright yellow (MC), Gold (A), Light blue (B).

Needles One pair size 6 (4mm) for smaller mittens OR size 7 (4.5mm) for larger mittens, *or size to obtain gauge.*

Extras Stitch holders.

Gauge 22 sts and 30 rows to 4" (10cm) over St st using size 6 (4mm) needles and sport weight yarn.

20 sts and 26 rows to 4" (10cm) over St st using size 7 (4.5mm) needles and worsted weight yarn.

EDITOR'S NOTE Use smaller needles and sport weight yarn for smaller sized puppets. Use larger needles and worsted weight yarn for larger sized puppets.

DRAGON

**With MC, cast on 36 sts. Work 18 rows in k2, p2 rib. Work 16 rows in St st.

Divide for jaw of puppet

Next row (RS) K18 and place them on hold; k rem 18 sts. **Next row** Purl 18. Work 18 rows more in St st over 18 sts.

*Shape tip: Row 1 K1, ssk, k to last 3 sts, k2tog, k1—16 sts. **Rows 2 and 4** Purl. **Row 3** Rep row 1—14 sts.

Row 5 Rep row 1—12 sts. **Row 6** P1, p2tog, p to last 3 sts, ssp, p1—10 sts. **Row 7** Rep row 1—8 sts.

Row 8 Rep row 6—6 sts. **Row 9** K1, ssk, k2tog, k1—4 sts. **Row 10** P1, p2tog, p1—3 sts. **Row 11** S2KP2. Fasten off.*

Thumb section (lower jaw of puppet)

With WS facing and MC, p across 18 sts on hold. Work 8 rows more in St st. Rep from* to * (shape tip) above.

Palm (inner, upper jaw)

With A, cast on 17 sts. **Row 1** K6, [p1, k1] 3 times, k5. **Row 2** P6, [k1, p1] 3 times, p5. **Rows 3-20** Rep rows 1-2. (*)Cont in pat, dec 1 st each end as for tip, every RS row twice, then every row until 5 sts rem. **Next row** (RS) K2tog, p1, k2tog—3 sts. **Next Row** S2PP2—1 st. Fasten off.(*)

Palm (lower, inner jaw)

With RS facing and A, pick up and k 15 sts across cast-on edge of upper jaw section, omitting first and last st. **Row 1** (WS) P5, [k1, p1] 3 times, p4. **Row 2** K5, [p1, k1] 3 times, k4. **Rows 3-11** Rep rows 1-2, end with row 1. Rep from (*) to (*) of Palm (upper jaw).

Finishing

Sew side seam until divided for jaw. Sew palm to finger and thumb sections (longer section to upper jaw, shorter section to lower jaw).**

Dragon spikes

With B, cast on 5 sts. **Rows 1-7** Knit and inc 1 st at end of rows 1, 3, 5 and 7—9 sts. **Rows 8-14** Knit and dec 1 st at beg of rows 8, 10, 12 and 14—5 sts.

Rows 15-29 Knit and beg with row 15, inc 1 st at end of every odd-numbered row—13 sts.

Rows 30-44 Knit and beg with row 30, dec 1 st at beg of every even-numbered row—5 sts.

Rep rows 1-14. Bind off rem sts. Fold in half and using photo as guide, sew spikes in position. With C, embroider eyes.

WHALE

Work as for Dragon from** to **.

Spout Using photo as guide, use MC to embroider large yarn loops to top of mitten. With B, embroider eyes.

KITTEN

Work as for Dragon from ** to **.

Make ears Fold felt in half and cut 2 pieces, each 1" square. Fold in half to form triangle, sew open sides of triangle and using photo as guide, sew to mitten. With B, embroider eyes.

PUPPY

Work as for Dragon from ** to **.

Ears (make 2) With B, cast on 10 sts. K 14 rows. K 6 rows more and dec 1 st at beg of each row. Bind off rem sts. Using photo as guide, sew ears to mitten. With C, embroider eyes and nose.

PONY

Work as for Dragon from** to **.

Mane Using photo as guide, embroider large loops to mitten with B. With C, embroider eyes.

GOLDFISH

With MC, cast on 36 sts. **Rows 1-18** Work in k2, p2 rib. **Rows 19-34** Beg with a k row, work in St st.

Divide for jaw

Row 35 (RS) K18 and place them on hold, k rem 18 sts. **Row 36-54** Beg with a p row, work in St st.

*Shape tip: **Row 1** K1, ssk, k to last 3 sts, k2tog, k1—16 sts. **Rows 2, 4 and 6** Purl. **Row 3** Rep row 1—14 sts. **Row 5** Rep row 1—12 sts. Cont to dec 2 sts every RS row until 4 sts rem. Purl 1 row. **Next row** K1, ssk, k2tog, k1—4 sts. **Next row** P1, p2tog, p1—3 sts. **Next row** S2KP2. Fasten off.*

Thumb section (lower jaw of puppet)

With WS facing and MC, p across 18 sts on holder. Work 8 rows more in St st. Rep from* to * (shape tip) above.

Palm (inner, upper jaw)

With MC, cast on 17 sts. **Row 1** K6, [p1, k1] 3 times, k5. **Row 2** P6, [k1, p1] 3 times, p5. **Rows 3-20** Rep rows 1-2. (*) Cont in pat, dec 1 st each side every RS row as for tip until 5 sts rem. **Next row** (RS) K2tog, p1, k2tog—3 sts. **Next row** S2PP2. Fasten off.(*)

Palm (lower, inner jaw)

With RS facing and MC, pick up and k15 sts across cast-on edge of upper jaw section, omitting first and last st. **Row 1** (WS) P5, [k1, p1] 3 times, p4. **Row 2** (RS) K5, [p1, k1] 3 times, k4. **Rows 3-11** Rep rows 1-2, end with row 1. Rep from (*) to (*) above.

Finishing

Sew side seam until divided for jaw. Sew palm to finger and thumb sections (longer section to upper jaw, shorter section to lower jaw).

Fins: Small (make 2) With A, cast on 6 sts. K 4 rows. K 2 rows more and dec 1 st at beg of each row. Bind off rem 4 sts. **Large** (make 1) With A, cast on 18 sts. K 3 rows. **Next row** K9, k into front and back of next st, k to last 4 sts, turn. K to last 4 sts, turn. K to end. K 2 rows more over all sts. Bind off.

Using photo as guide, sew fins into position. With B, embroider eyes.

These two-needle mittens are modeled on one of the patterns I used when learning to knit. Over the years at my children's requests, I have made brown and gold striped tigers, sharks, bumblebees (yellow with black stripes on the cuffs). And when they no longer wanted puppets—regular mittens.

Bobbled Rainbow Hats

ADVANCED BEGINNER

While vacationing in San Diego, I was taken by beautiful bright cotton yarns. I bought one of each color, not knowing what I was going to do with them. Intrigued by a bobble edge described in Kristin Nicholas' *Festive Family Footwear* booklet, I decided to use it to form the beginning of this hat.

Cotton hats are great for kids, especially infants, because the itch factor is reduced and they are washer friendly. A variation of the same hat was made with yarn dyed with Kool Aid with my kindergarten Daisy Girl Scouts. Beginners can tackle this project— give them a hand with the bobbles! And even the youngest children can help dye the yarn that is used to create hats you are going to knit for them.

Size Cotton hat Circumference approx 14". **Wool hat** Circumference approx 18".

Yarns Cotton hat 1 ball (each 1¾oz/50g) sport or worsted weight cotton each in 5 colors. **Wool hat** Approx 8 oz of worsted weight wool in White.

Needles Cotton hat Size 6 (4mm) circular needle, 16"/40cm long and double-pointed needles (dpn), *or size to obtain gauge.* **Wool hat** Size 8 (5mm) needle, circular and dpn, *or size to obtain gauge.*

Extras Stitch markers.

Gauge 20 sts and 28 rows to 4" (10cm) over St st using size 6 (4mm) needles and cotton yarn.

18 sts and 26 rows to 4" (10cm) over St st using size 8 (5mm) needles and worsted weight yarn.

COTTON HAT

With circular needle and A, cast on 72 sts. **Make bobbles: Row 1** *K3, make bobble as foll: In next st, work (k1, yo, k1, yo, k1) to make 5 sts from 1. Turn and k5. Turn and p5. Turn and k5. Turn and sl 2nd, then 3rd, then 4th , then 5th st one at a time over first st on right needle. Rep from* across. Work in rnds as foll:

Rnd 2 Place marker and join, being careful not to twist sts and knit.

Rnds 3-5 Knit.

Rnds 6-7 With B, knit. **Rnd 8** With B, *k2tog, yo; rep from* around. **Rnds 9-10** With B, knit.

Rnd 11 With C, knit. **Rnds 12-15** With C, purl.

Rnds 16-20 With D, knit.

Rnd 21 With E, knit. **Rnds 22-25** With E, purl.

Rnds 26-30 With D, knit.

Rnd 31 With C, knit. **Rnds 32-35** With C, purl.

Rnds 36-40 With B, knit.

Rnd 41 With A, knit. **Rnds 42 and 44** With A, purl. **Rnd 43** With A, *p3, make bobble in next st; rep from* around.

Rnd 45 With D, knit and place a marker after every 12th st. Make sure the marker for the beg of the rnd is different than the other markers.

Rnd 46 With D, knit and work k2tog after each marker. **Rnd 47** With D, knit.

Rep rnds 46-47 until 6 sts rem. Change to dpn when necessary.

Work I-cord

Place the 6 sts on 1 dpn. With 2nd dpn, *knit. Do not turn work; sl sts to beg of needle. Rep from* for approx 3½". Draw the sts tog and fasten off. Tie knot in I-cord. Sew edges of first (bobble) row tog.

WOOL HAT

EDITOR'S NOTE See p. 67 for general instructions on dyeing with Kool Aid. Dye a variety of colors (referred to as A, B, C, D and E in pattern) and use photo as guide for color placement.

With circular needle and A, cast on 72 sts. **Make bobbles: Row 1** *K3, make bobble as foll: In next st, work (k1, yo, k1, yo, k1) to make 5 sts from 1. Turn and k5. Turn and p5. Turn and k5. Turn and sl 2nd, then 3rd, then 4th , then 5th st one at a time over first st on right needle. Rep from* across. Work in rnds as foll:

Rnd 2 Place marker and join, being careful not to twist sts and knit.

Rnds 3-4 Knit.

Rnd 5 With B, knit. **Rnd 6** With B, *k2tog, yo; rep from* around. **Rnd 7** With B, knit.

Rnd 8 With C, knit. **Rnds 9-11** With C, purl.

Rnds 12-15 With D, knit.

Rnd 16 With E, knit. **Rnds 17-20** With E, purl.

Rnds 21-24 With D, knit.

Rnd 25 With C, knit. **Rnds 26-28** With C, purl.

Rnds 29-32 With D, knit.

Rnd 33 With A, knit. **Rnd 34** With A, *k3, make bobble in next st; rep from* around.

Rnds 35-36 With A, knit.

Rnd 37 With B, knit and place a marker after every 12th st. Make sure the marker for the beg of the rnd is different than the other markers.

Rnd 38 With B, knit and work k2tog after each marker. **Rnd 39** With B, knit. Rep rnds 38-39 until 5 sts rem between markers. Change to dpn when necessary. Then k2tog after each marker every rnd until there are 6 sts left. Work I-cord (see cotton hat) for approx 4½". Tie knot in I-cord. Sew edges of first (bobble) row tog.

Cotton hat

Kool Aid dyed wool hat

A Matched Set

INTERMEDIATE

When knitting for our daughter Bethany, I involve her in the selection of colors and fibers. She loves to wear fun, bright-colored clothes.

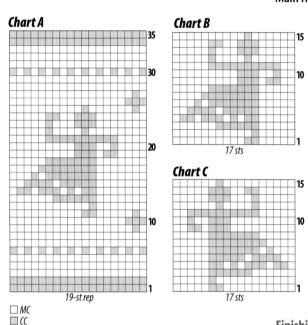

Chart A

35

30

20

10

1

19-st rep

□ MC
▨ CC

Chart B

15

10

1

17 sts

Chart C

15

10

1

17 sts

Measurements **Hat** Circumference approx 21" (to fit child's medium/large head). **Scarf** Approx 6½" by 36½".

Yarns 8 balls sport weight yarn (each 1¾oz/50g, approx 136yd/124m) in Purple multi (MC) and 1 ball in Medium pink (CC).

Needles In size 7 (4.5mm): set of double pointed needles (dpn), *or size to obtain gauge.* Two circular needles, each 16"/40cm long. 2 dpn in size 6 (4mm) for I-cord.

Extras Size G/6 (4.5mm) crochet hook. Stitch holder and markers. 48 medium pink plastic pony beads.

Gauge **Hat and scarf** 22 sts and 30 rows to 4" (10cm) over St st using size 7 (4.5mm) needles and MC.

Mittens 19 sts and 28 rows to 4" (10cm) over St st using 2 strands of MC held tog and size 7 (4.5mm) needles.

HAT
Lining
With crochet hook and CC, work chain cast-on as foll: chain 114. With size 7 circular needle and MC, knit up 1 st in each chain, inserting needle into back loops of crochet—114 sts. Place marker and join, being careful not to twist sts. K 40 rnds. P 2 rnds (turning ridge). K 3 rnds.

Main Hat
Beg Chart A: Rnd 1 Work 19-st rep of Chart A around. Work through chart rnd 35. Cut CC. With MC, k 3 rnds.

Join lining and main hat
Open CC chain sts one by one and sl sts onto 2nd circular needle—114 sts. Fold to inside at turning ridge. K2tog (1 st from each needle) around—114 sts. With MC, p 2 rnds, then k 1 rnd.

Shape crown
Rnd 1 *K8, S2KP2, k8; rep from* around—102 sts. **Rnd 2** Knit. **Rnd 3** *K7, S2KP2, k7; rep from* around—90 sts. **Rnd 4** Knit. Change to size 7 dpns. Cont to dec as established every other rnd until 18 sts rem. Sl next 3 sts onto size 6 dpn and work I-cord for approx 4". Using up 3 sts each, make 5 more I-cords. Secure ends and slip one bead onto each I-cord, making knot at I-cord end. Secure opening at center of hat.

Scarf
With crochet hook and CC, chain 76. With size 7 circular needle and MC, knit up 1 st in each chain, inserting needle into back loops of crochet—76 sts. Place marker and join, being careful not to twist sts. K 10 rnds.

Beg Chart A: Rnd 1 Work 19-st rep of Chart A around. Work through chart rnd 35. Cut CC. With MC, knit for approx 34" more.

Beg Chart A: Rnd 35 Work 19-st rep of row 35 of Chart A. Working chart backwards, work to chart row 1. Cut CC. With MC, k 10 rnds.

Finishing
I-Cord fringes
Slip first 38 sts onto 2nd circular needle. With size 6 dpn and MC, *k2tog (1 st from 2nd needle and 1 st from first needle), rep from* once more—2 sts on dpn. Using dpn, work a 2-st I-Cord for approx 6". Cut yarn. Slide bead onto I-Cord and secure, making knot. In same way, cont to work 2-st I-Cords until all sts are used up—19 I-Cords.
Work I-cord fringe as above.

MITTENS
Right Hand
With size 7 circular needle and 2 strands of MC held tog, cast on 42 sts. Work back and forth in rows as foll: **Row 1 (RS) *K3, p1; rep from* to last 2 sts, k2. **Row 2** (WS) K1, *k1, p3; rep from* to last st, k1. Rep last 2 rows until piece measures 3½" from beg, end with a WS row. **Next row** K2, *k3, k2tog; rep from* across—34 sts. Work 3 rows in St st. **Next (eyelet) row** (RS) K2; *yo, k2tog, k2; rep from * across row. Work 3 rows in St st.
Shape thumb gusset: Row 1 (RS) K16, place marker, M1, k2, M1, place 2nd marker, k16—36 sts. **Row 2** Purl. **Row 3** K16, M1, k4, M1, k16—38 sts. **Row 4** Purl. Cont to inc 2 sts every RS row to shape gusset until there are 10 sts between markers. **Next row** P42. **Next row** (RS) K16, slip next 10 sts onto holder, cast on 2 sts, k16 sts—34 sts. **Next row** Purl.**
Beg Chart B: Row 1 (RS) Work 17 sts of chart, place marker, with MC, k to end. **Row 2** (WS) With MC, p to marker, then work chart row 2. In same way, work through chart row 15. **Next row** (WS) With MC, purl.

Shape tip: Row 1 (RS) K1, [k1, ssk, k10, k2tog, k1] twice, k1—30 sts. **Row 2** P1, [p1, p2tog, p8, S2PP2, p1] twice, p1—26 sts. In same way, cont to dec 4 sts every row until 10 sts rem. Cut yarn leaving 20" tail, slip through 10 sts, tighten and sew side seam.

Thumb

Slip 5 sts from holder onto first dpn and rem 5 sts onto 2nd dpn. Join yarn and k across these 10 sts with 3rd dpn, then pick up and k 4 sts along base of thumb—14 sts. Join and k in rnds for 1½". **Next rnd** K1, [k2tog, k1] 4 times, k1—10 sts. **Next rnd** [K2tog] 5 times—5 sts. Cut yarn, leaving a 4" tail. Draw tail through rem sts, tighten and fasten off.

Left Hand

Work as for Right Hand from** to **. **Beg Chart C: Row 1** (RS) With MC, k17, place marker, work 17 sts of chart. **Row 2** (WS) Work chart row 2 with MC, p to end. In same way, work through chart row 15. **Next row** (WS) With MC, purl. Shape tip and make thumb as for right hand.

I-Cord drawstrings (make 2)

With size 6 dpn and MC, cast on 3 sts. Work I-cord for approx 18". Cut yarn. Thread I-Cord through eyelet row of mitten. Slip beads onto ends of I-Cord and knot.

The North wind doth blow!

The North wind doth blow,

And we shall have snow,

And what will poor robin do then,

Poor thing?

He'll sit in a barn.

And keep himself warm,

And hide his head under his wing,

Poor thing.

Winter/Outdoors

Ana's Lopi Coat

EXPERIENCED

I designed this coat for my granddaughter, using yarn inherited from my mother.
Elizabeth Zimmermann's percentage system for seamless sweaters in *Knitting Without Tears* heavily influenced the shaping in this coat.
I used color patterns from Sheila McGregor's *The Traditional Book of Fair Isle Knitting.*

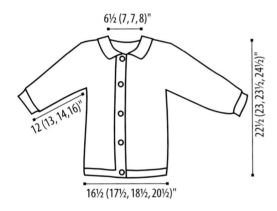

6½ (7, 7, 8)"

22½ (23, 23½, 24½)"

12 (13, 14, 16)"

16½ (17½, 18½, 20½)"

Sizes 4 (6, 8, 10). Shown in size 6.

Measurements Chest (buttoned) 33 (35, 37, 41)". Length 22½ (23, 23½, 24½)".

Yarn Chunky (Lopi-type) weight: approx 10 (10, 12, 13) oz in Dark gray; 4 (4, 6, 6) oz each in Mauve and Light gray; 3 (3, 4, 4) oz each in White and Claret and small amount of Turquoise.

Needles One each sizes 7 and 10 (4.5 and 6mm) circular needles, 24"/60cm, *or size to obtain gauge.* Sizes 7 and 10 double pointed needles (dpn). **Extras** Stitch holders and markers. Five ⅝" buttons. Size G/6 (4.5 mm) crochet hook.

Gauge 16 sts and 18 rows to 4" (10cm) in St st and Fair Isle pat using size 10 (6mm) needles.

EDITOR'S NOTE The body of this garment is knit circularly to the underarm with a steek at centerfront. The sleeves are also knit circularly to the underarm, then united with the body into a circular yoke.

Body

With size 10 (24") needle and scrap yarn, cast on 131 (139, 147, 163) sts. Change to white. Place marker and join, being careful not to twist sts, and k 1 rnd. The first 3 sts after the marker are the steek sts. Beg with rnd 1, work chart pat through rnd 61, working chart reps around as necessary and end at marker. Place all sts on hold.

Sleeves

With size 7 dpn and MC, cast on 26 (28, 30, 32) sts and divide evenly over 3 dpn. Place marker, join and work 1½" in circular garter st (p 1 rnd, k 1 rnd), end just before marker on last rnd. Place 2nd marker on needle, then M1 (inc'd st is between markers)—27 (29, 31, 33) sts. Change to size 10 dpn. On body, beg at sts on hold and measure down 10½ (11½, 12½, 14½)". Beg with that row of chart pat and work through chart rnd 61, AT SAME TIME, inc 1 st each side of markers (working incs and marked st into chart pat) every 4th row 8 (8, 9, 10) times—43 (45, 49, 53) sts; piece measures approx 12 (13, 14, 16)" from beg. Place 5 (5, 6, 6) sts before and after joining marker on hold. Place rem 33 (35, 37, 41) sts on hold.

Yoke

Join body and sleeves: Next rnd (RS) Working chart rnd 62, with RS facing and size 10 (24") needle, beg at marker and k3 steek sts, then k27 (29, 30, 34) sts (right front), place next 10 (10, 12, 12) sts of body on hold (underarm), k33 (35, 37, 41) sts of first sleeve, then k next 54 (58, 60, 68) sts (back), place next 10 (10, 12, 12) sts of body on hold (underam), k33 (35, 37, 41) sts of 2nd sleeve, k to marker (left front)—177 (189, 197, 221) sts. Work through chart rnd 77. **Next (dec) rnd** Working chart rnd 78, work 3 steek sts, *k1, k2tog; rep from* around, end k0 (0, 2, 2)—119 (127, 133, 149) sts. Work through chart rnd 88. Rep dec rnd across chart rnd 89, end k2 (1, 1, 2)—81 (86, 90, 101) sts. Work 1½ (1½, 2, 2)" even in chart pat, working chart motifs from beg of chart as necessary. Rep dec rnd, end k0 (2, 0, 2)—55 (59, 61, 69) sts. Work even until yoke measures 7½ (8, 8, 9)" from underarm (measure straight up from underarm), end at marker. Place all sts on hold.

Finishing

Block piece. Secure steek sts by machine or by hand and cut centerfront. Weave underarms tog.

Collar

With RS facing, size 7 circular needle and MC, k across 52 (56, 58, 66) sts at neck edge. Turn and k 1 rnd.

Shape back neck Work in short rows as foll: **Row 1** (RS) K39 (42, 44, 50) sts, wrap next st, turn (W/T). **Row 2** K15 (16, 16, 18) sts, W/T. **Row 3** K17 (18, 18, 20) sts, W/T. **Row 4** K19 (20, 20, 22) sts, W/T. **Row 5** K21 (22, 22, 24) sts, W/T. **Row 6** K to end, turn. **Row 7** K across all sts. Cont in garter st until collar measures approx 3" along centerfront edge. Bind off all sts.

Lower band

Remove scrap yarn at lower edge and sl sts to size 7 (24") needle. With MC, k across first row and dec 12 (13, 14, 16) sts evenly across—116 (123, 130, 144) sts. Work 1½ (1½, 2, 2)" in garter st. Bind off loosely.

Buttonband

With RS facing, size 7 (24") needle and MC, pick up and k evenly from left neck edge to lower edge. Work 1" in garter st. Place 5 markers for buttons on band, the first approx 1" from top of band, the last approx 2" from lower edge, and 3 others spaced evenly between.

Buttonhole band

Work to correspond to button-band, working buttonholes

when band is ½"as foll: Bind off 2 sts opposite each marker. On next row, cast on 2 sts over bound-off sts of previous row. Sew buttons on.

■ Dark gray
■ Mauve
□ Light gray
■ Claret
□ White
■ Turquoise

Hey, Frosty!

INTERMEDIATE

The inspiration
for my snowman sweater
came after taking a class on kids' knits
with designer Debbie Bliss (my hero).

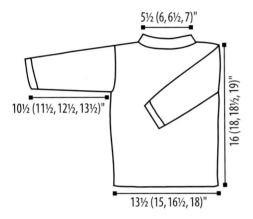

5½ (6, 6½, 7)"

10½ (11½, 12½, 13½)"

16 (18, 18½, 19)"

13½ (15, 16½, 18)"

Sizes 2 (4, 6, 8). Shown in size 8.

Finished Measurements Chest 27 (30, 33, 36)". Length 16 (18, 18½, 19)".

Yarn 6 (6, 7, 8) balls worsted weight yarn (each 1¾oz/50g, approx 110yd/100m) in Blue (MC). 4 balls in White (A). 1 ball each in Red (B), Brown (C) and Rust (D).

Needles For size 2 only One pair each sizes 6 and 8 (4 and 4.5mm), *or size needed to obtain gauge.*

For sizes 4, 6, 8 only One pair each sizes 7 and 9 (4 and 5mm), *or size needed to obtain gauge.*

Extras Stitch markers. Bobbins. Nine buttons in assorted sizes and colors.

Gauge For size 2 only 20 sts and 28 rows to 4"/10cm in St st using size 8 (4.5mm) needles.

For sizes 4, 6, 8 only 18 sts and 24 rows to 4"/10cm in St st using size 9 (5mm) needles.

EDITOR'S NOTE Use separate bobbins for large blocks of color. Remember to twist colors on WS to prevent holes.

Back

With smaller needles and A, cast on 66 (66, 74, 78) sts. Beg with a p row, work 6 rows in St st. **Rib row 1** (WS) *P2, k2; rep from* across, end p2. **Rib row 2** *K2, p2; rep from* across, end k2. Rep last 2 rows 4 times more and inc 2 (2, 0, 2) sts evenly across—68 (68, 74, 80) sts. Change to larger needles. P 1 row. **Beg Chart 1: Row 1** (RS) Beg and end as indicated for your size, k row 1 across. Work to top of chart. With MC only, cont in St st until piece measures 16 (18, 18½, 19)" from beg (measure piece with edge rolled). Bind off 20 (20, 22, 24) sts at beg of next 2 rows. Place rem 28 (28, 30, 32) sts on hold.

Front

Cast on and work St st, rib and inc as for back. Change to larger needles. P 1 row. **Beg Chart 2: Row 1** (RS) Beg and end as indicated for your size, k row 1 across. Work to top of chart, then work 4 rows more with MC. Piece measures approx 14½ (16½, 16½, 16½)" from beg (measure piece with edge rolled). Cont with MC only.

Shape neck

Next row (RS) K24 (24, 26, 28) sts, place next 20 (20, 22, 24) sts on hold, join a 2nd ball of yarn and work to end. Working both sides at same time, dec 1 st at each neck edge every other row 4 times—20 (20, 22, 24) sts rem each side. Work even until piece measures same as back to shoulder. Bind off all sts.

Sleeves

With smaller needles and MC, cast on 34 (34, 38, 38) sts. Work in St st and rib as for back and inc 2 (2, 2, 4) sts evenly across last row—36 (36, 40, 42) sts. Change to larger needles. P 1 row. Cont in St st, AT SAME TIME, inc 1 st each side every 6th row 9 (9, 10, 11) times—54 (54, 60, 64) sts. Work even until piece measures 10½ (11½, 12½, 13½)" from beg (measured with edge rolled). Bind off all sts loosely.

Finishing

Block pieces. Sew right shoulder.

Neckband

With RS facing and smaller needles, beg at left front neck and *pick up and k8 (8, 10, 12) sts to sts on hold*, k20 (20, 22, 24) sts from front neck, rep between*'s once, k28 (28, 30, 32) sts from back neck—64 (64, 72, 80) sts. K 1 row, then p 2 rows. **Rib row 1** (RS) *K2, p2; rep from*. Rep last row 11 times more. Beg with a k row, work 4 rows in St st. Bind off all sts. Sew left shoulder and neckband, reversing seam on final 4 rows of St st. Place markers 5½ (6, 6½, 7)" down from shoulders on front and back. Sew top of sleeves between markers. Sew side and sleeve seams. Using photo as guide, sew buttons as desired for eyes, mouth and along front of snowman.

Chart 1

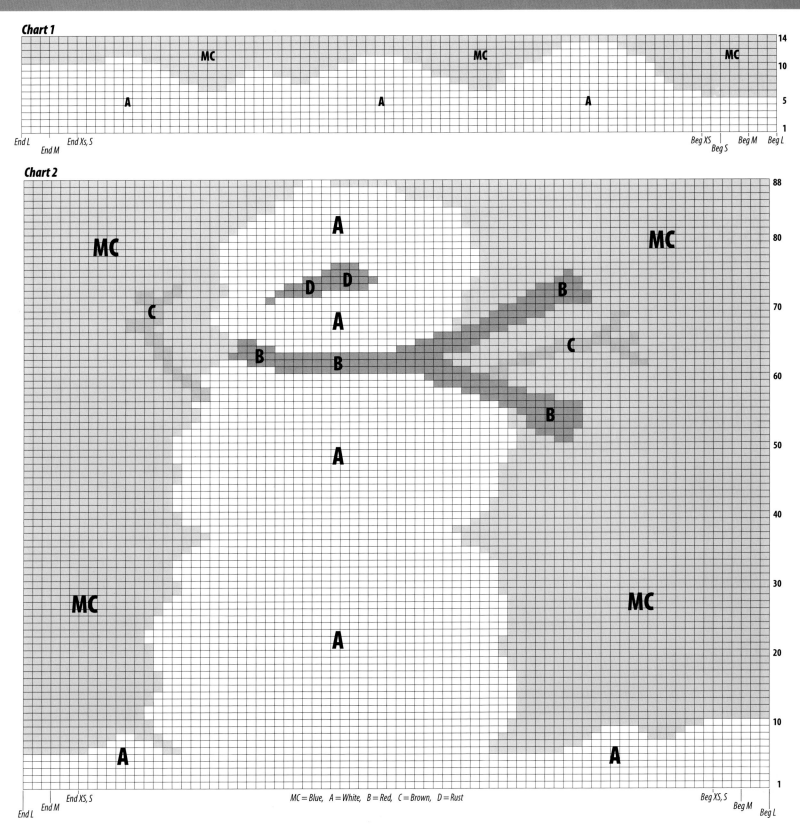

MC = Blue, A = White, B = Red, C = Brown, D = Rust

Snowflakes

INTERMEDIATE

Besides designing knitwear, I am also a partner in a computer consulting company, specializing in system design and analysis for scientific applications. If I had one bit of advice to tell people who were knitting for children, it would be to let them help in the design and/or color choices for the garment. Several of my friends have small children, 5 years and under. You would not believe how particular they are already about the clothes they wear!

5½ (6, 6, 6½)"

11 (12, 13, 13)"

15 (16, 18, 19)"

14 (15, 16, 17)"

Sizes 2 (4, 6, 8). Shown in size 2.

Measurements Chest 28 (30, 32, 34)". Length 15 (16, 18, 19)".

Yarn 6 (7, 9, 10) balls worsted weight yarn (each 1¾oz/50g, approx 110yd/100m) in Navy (MC). 4 (5, 6, 6) balls Ivory (CC).

Needles One pair each sizes 6 and 8 (4 and 5mm) needles, *or size to obtain gauge.*

Extras Stitch holders and markers. One ⅝" button. Size F/5 (4mm) crochet hook.

Gauge 20 sts and 28 rows to 4" (10cm) over St st using size 8 (5mm) needles and MC.

Back

With smaller needles and CC, cast on 70 (76, 80, 86) sts. K 2 rows. Change to MC. Work 10 rows in k2, p2 rib. Change to larger needles. Purl 1 row and inc 1 st at beg of row—71 (77, 81, 87) sts. **Beg body chart: Row 1** (RS) K0 (3, 5, 8) MC, reading chart from right to left, work 71 sts of chart row 1, end k0 (3, 5, 8) MC. **Row 2** (WS) P0 (3, 5, 8) MC, reading chart from left to right, work 71 sts of chart row 2, end p0 (3,5, 8) MC. Cont chart pat as established, working 0 (3, 5, 8) sts outside of chart pat in St st with MC, and rep last 10 rows of chart as necessary, until piece measures 12 (13, 15, 16)" from beg, end with a WS row.

Split for back neck opening

Next row (RS) Cont chart pat, work 35 (38, 40, 43) sts, bind off next st, work to end. Working both sides with separate balls of yarn, work chart pat (and rep last 10 rows of chart as necessary) until piece is 15 (16, 18, 19)" from beg. Place the rem sts each side on hold.

Front

Work as for back until piece is 3½" less than back to shoulder, end with a WS row.

Shape neck

Next row (RS) Cont chart pat, work 29 (31, 32, 34) sts, place next 13 (15, 17, 19) sts on hold, join 2nd balls of yarn and work to end. Working both sides at same time, bind off from each neck edge 3 sts once, 2 sts once. Dec 1 st at each neck edge every other row twice. Work even on rem 22 (24, 25, 27) sts until piece measures same as back to shoulder. Place all sts on hold.

Sleeves

With smaller needles and CC, cast on 34 (40, 40, 44) sts. K 2 rows. Change to MC. Work 8 rows in k2, p2 rib. Change to larger needles. Purl 1 row and inc 1 st at beg of row—35 (41, 41, 45) sts. **Beg sleeve chart** Beg with row 1, work chart pat, working first and last 0 (3, 5, 8) sts with MC in St st as for back, and cont to work alternating cross motif as established after row 26, AT SAME TIME, inc 1 st each side (working incs into chart pat) every 4th row 15 (15, 10, 10) times, every 6th row 0 (0,

Body chart

Note Neck slit on chart shows stitch placement only. Begin the neck slit as indicated in written pat. ➤

5, 5) times—65 (71, 71, 75) sts. Work even until piece measures 11 (12, 13, 13)" from beg. Bind off all sts.

Finishing

Block pieces. With RS facing, join shoulders using 3-needle bind-off.

Neckband

With RS facing, smaller needles and MC, beg at left back neck edge and pick up and k approx 82 (86, 90, 94) sts evenly around to right back neck edge (including sts on hold at centerfront). Work 8 rows in k2, p2 rib. Change to CC. K 2 rows. Bind off.

With CC, join yarn to top of neckband and work 1 row sc, then 1 row reverse sc around center back opening, making a loop at the top of the opening for a buttonhole. Sew button into place.

Sleeve chart

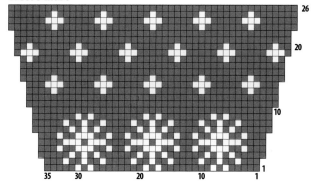

Snowflake Pullover

INTERMEDIATE

EDITOR'S NOTE This garment is knit entirely in the round. The body is knit circularly to the underarms. The sleeves are also knit circularly to the underarm, then joined with the body into a circularly knit yoke. Change to dpn or longer circular needle as required.

Body

With size 7 (24") circular needle, cast on 120 (130, 140) sts. Being careful not to twist sts, place marker (pm), join and work rnds 1-10 of Chart A. Change to size 9 circular needle. Work to top of chart, then work in St st (k every rnd) until piece measures 8 (8½, 9)" from beg, end at joining marker. **Next rnd** Bind off 4 sts, k until there are 51 (56, 61) sts on right needle (front), bind off next 9 sts (underarm), k until there are 51 (56, 61) sts on right needle (back), bind off rem 5 sts (underarm).

Sleeves

With size 7 (size 9, size 9) dpn, cast on 30 sts and divide evenly over 3 dpn. Being careful not to twist sts, pm, join and work rnds 1-10 of Chart B, inc and marking seam st as indicated. **For size 2** change to larger dpn. **For all sizes** work to top of chart and inc as indicated—42 sts. Cont in St st and inc 1 st each side of seam st every 6th row 6 times—54 sts. Work even until piece measures 8½ (9½, 10½)" from beg, end 4 sts before marked seam st. **Next rnd** Bind off 9 sts, place rem 45 sts on hold. In same way, make 2nd sleeve.

Join sleeves and body

With RS facing, join yarn and k51 (56, 61) sts of body (front), pm, k45 sts of one sleeve, pm, k51 (56, 61) sts of body (back), then k45 sts of 2nd sleeve—192 (202, 212) sts. Place joining marker, join and work in St st for 1 (1½, 2)" even. **Next (dec) rnd** Dec 4 (9, 14) sts evenly across front, 4 sts evenly across sleeve, 4 (9, 14) sts evenly across back and 4 sts evenly across 2nd sleeve—176 sts (41 sts on each sleeve, 47 sts on front, 47 sts on back). Beg as indicated, work Chart C, changing to smaller needle chart rnd 39. Work to top of chart. Do not bind off.

Finishing

With crochet hook, work one row of crochet around neck as foll: *Work sl st into next 3 sts on needle, ch 3 (picot over k st), sl st into same stitch, work sl st into next 2 sts on needle. Rep from* around. Sew body and sleeves tog at underarm. Block piece.

I design knitwear and own a publishing house specializing in patterns for handknitters. In addition, I teach knitting locally and nationally, including classes in designing for children.

My other interests include spinning, medieval literature, ballet and modern dance, and breastfeeding advocacy.

When I can steal time from my professional knitting commitments, I knit for my two daughters, ages 6 and 9, who are especially appreciative of handknit wool socks.

When knitting for children, it's important to use good materials. You never know which garment, blanket or toy will turn out to be a favorite for one child, or for the whole family, and be passed on to generations of children. If it is well-loved, it will be very well-worn, and must be made out of the best materials to stand up to all that loving over the years."

Sizes 2 (4, 6). Shown in size 2.

Measurements Chest 26½ (29, 31)". Length 15 (16, 17)".

Yarn 6 (7, 8) balls worsted weight yarn (each 1¾ oz/50g, approx 110yd/100m) in White.

Needles Size 9 (5.5mm) circular needle, 24"/60cm, *or size to obtain gauge.* Size 7 (4.5mm) circular needle, 16"/40cm and 24"/60cm. One set each sizes 7 and 9 (4.5 and 5.5mm) double-pointed needles (dpn).

Extras Stitch holders and markers. Size C/2 (2.5mm) crochet hook.

Gauge 18 sts and 26 rows to 4" (10cm) in St st using size 9 (5.5mm) needles.

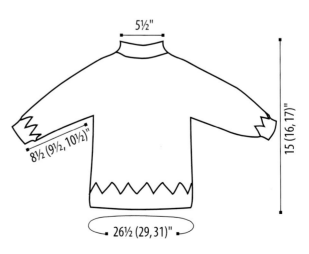

Chart A

19
15
10
5
3
1

10-st rep

Chart B

19
15
10
5
3
1

seam st
10-st rep

Chart C

55
50
45
40
35
30
25
20
15
10
5

22-st rep
beg

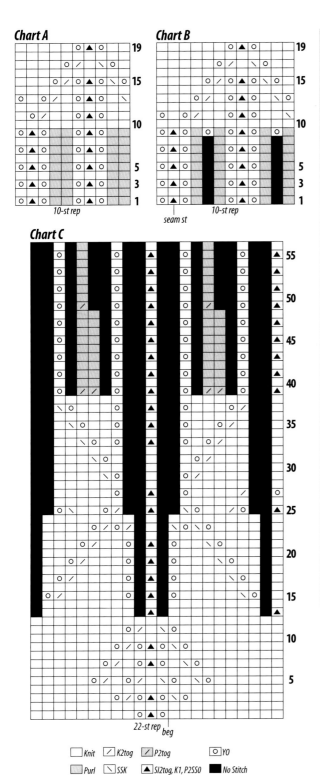

☐ Knit   ╱ K2tog   ╱ P2tog   ◉ YO
▦ Purl   ╲ SSK   ▲ Sl2tog, K1, P2SS0   ■ No Stitch

Snowy Pines

INTERMEDIATE

EDITOR'S NOTE This garment is knit in one piece to the underarm, then divided into fronts and back. When working charts, remember to twist colors on WS to avoid holes. Carry yarns loosely along on WS of work. For ease in working, circle numbers for your size.

Body

With smaller needles and A, cast on 115 (123, 143, 155, 175, 183) sts. Change to MC. **Rib row 1** (WS) *P3, k1; rep from*, end p3. **Rib row 2** (RS) *K3, p1; rep from*, end k3. Rep last 2 rows until rib measures 1 (½, 2, 2, 2, 2½)" from beg, end with row 2. Change to larger needles. **Next row** (WS) Purl and dec 2 (0, 0, 2, 2, 0) sts evenly across—113 (123, 143, 153, 173, 183) sts. **Beg Tree Chart: Row 1** With MC, work 10-st rep across, end k3 MC. **Next row** P3 MC, then work chart row 2 across. In same way, work through chart row 15. **For sizes 1 and 8** P 1 row and inc 1 st at beg and end of row—115 (175) sts. On row 1 of Snow Chart, work 12-st rep across, then end by working sts 1-7. **For sizes 2 and 10** P 1 row and dec 1 st—122 (182) sts. Work first and last st in St st with MC and work 12-st rep of Snow Chart across rem sts. **For sizes 4 and 6** P 1 row and Inc 1 (3) sts—144 (156) sts. Work 12-st rep of Snow Chart across. **For all sizes** Work through chart row 10. Work even in St st with MC until piece measures 7½ (9, 10, 10½, 12, 14)" from beg, end with a WS row.

Divide for fronts and back

Next row (RS) K27 (29, 34, 37, 42, 44), ssk, k2tog, k53 (56, 68, 74, 83, 86), ssk, k2tog, k to end. **Next row** (WS) P28 (30, 35, 38, 43, 45) sts (left front) and place all other sts on hold. Cont in St st on left front sts until piece measures 8½ (10, 11, 11½, 13, 15)" from beg, end with a WS row.

Shape V-neck

Next row (RS) Work to last 4 sts, ssk, k2. **Next row** Purl. In same way, dec 1 st at neck edge every other row 0 (1, 4, 1, 3, 2) times more, every 4th row 9 (9, 8, 11, 10, 12) times. Work even on rem 18 (19, 22, 25, 29, 30) sts until piece measures 13 (15, 16½, 17½, 19, 22)" from beg. Bind off all sts.

Back

Sl 55 (58, 70, 76, 85, 88) sts of back to needle. With WS facing and MC, p across back sts. Cont in St st until piece measures same as left front to shoulder. Bind off all sts.

Right front

Sl 28 (30, 35, 38, 43, 45) sts of right front to needle. With WS facing and MC, p across right front sts. Work even until piece measures same as left front to beg of V-neck shaping, end with a WS row. Shape V-neck and complete piece as for left front. Reverse neck shaping by working k2, k2tog at beg of RS rows.

My first knitting project was argyle socks in '54—I was going on 13 years old that summer. Mrs. Connell taught me and her daughter, Peg, to knit. I made every mistake possible, threw them away and began again. That pair came out just fine and I became a knitter for life. A knitting project is the first thing I pack for a trip. I cannot be without knitting. I started knitting "by the book," but 30 years ago Elizabeth Zimmermann changed my knitting life. It is virtually impossible for me to blindly follow a pattern. I now use the computer to design. The joy of knitting is in handling a good yarn, creating a useful, beautiful garment. I knit for my children and grandchildren and favor traditional styles with perfect finishing. This sweater is for my granddaughter Alaina.

Sizes 1 (2, 4, 6, 8, 10). Shown in size 2.

Measurements Chest (buttoned) 24 (26, 28, 30, 32, 36)". Length 13 (15, 16½, 17½, 19, 22)".

Yarn 5 (5, 6, 7, 9, 10) balls worsted weight yarn (each 1¾oz/50g, approx 110yd/100m) in Burgundy (MC); small amounts in Pine green (A) and White (B).

Needles One pair each sizes 6 and 8 (4 and 5mm) needles, or size to obtain gauge. Size 6 (4mm) circular needle, 24"/60cm long.

Extras Stitch holders and markers. Size D/3 (3mm) crochet hook. Five ⅜" buttons.

Gauge 20 sts and 28 rows to 4" (10cm) in St st using size 8 (5mm) needles and MC.

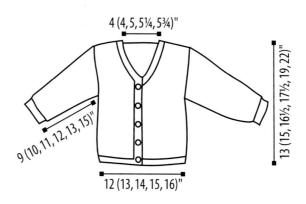

4 (4, 5, 5¼, 5¾)"

13 (15, 16½, 17½, 19, 22)"

9 (10, 11, 12, 13, 15)"

12 (13, 14, 15, 16)"

Sleeves

With smaller needles and A, cast on 38 (38, 41, 41, 41, 44) sts. Change to MC. **Rib row 1** (WS) *P2, k1; rep from*, end p2. **Rib row 2** *K2, p1; rep from*, end k2. Rep last 2 rows until rib measures 1 (1, 1½, 1½, 2, 2)" from beg, end with row 1. Change to larger needles. Cont in St st, AT SAME TIME, inc 1 st each side (working incs into St st) every 4th row 4 (3, 6, 5, 5, 7) times, every 6th row 6 (8, 7, 9, 9, 10) times—58 (60, 67, 69, 69, 78) sts. Work even until piece measures 9 (10, 11, 12, 13, 15)" from beg. Bind off all sts.

Finishing

Block pieces. Sew shoulder seams. Place 5 markers for buttonholes (on left front for boys, on right front for girls), the first and last approx ½" from lower edge and beg of V-neck shaping and 3 others spaced evenly between.

Front bands

With RS facing, circular needle and MC, beg at lower edge of right front and pick up and k approx 3 out of every 4 sts to beg of V-neck shaping, place marker, pick up and k in same way to beg of V-neck shaping on left front, place marker, pick up and k in same way to left front lower edge. Count sts from lower edge to markers on each front and on first knit row, inc or dec to get to same number. **Rows 1, 3, 5 and 7** (WS) Knit. **Rows 2 and 6** Knit and inc 1 st (k into front and back of st) after marker on right front and before marker on left front. **Row 4** Rep row 2 and work buttonholes (on right front for girls, on left front for boys) at markers as foll: yo, k2tog. **Row 8** With A, leaving a 10" tail at beg and end of row, knit and bind off at same time. With crochet hook, use tails and work sl st crochet along lower edges of bands. Sew top of sleeves into armholes. Sew sleeve seams. Sew buttons on.

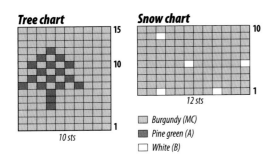

Tree chart

10 sts

Snow chart

12 sts

☐ Burgundy (MC)
■ Pine green (A)
☐ White (B)

Bog Jacket Variation

INTERMEDIATE

EDITOR'S NOTE   This jacket is constructed following Elizabeth Zimmermann's percentage system for bog jackets in *Knitting Around*. We have sized it using Ann's variations on classic techniques. The garment is knit in one piece to the underarm. Sleeve stitches are cast on and the sleeves and yoke are knit together, using short rows to shape the sleeves.

This jacket is basically constructed according to the bog jacket instructions in Elizabeth Zimmermann's *Knitting Around* with some modifications: 1) Phony seams at sides and shoulder line, 2) sleeves lengthened, 3) sleeves shaped with short rows, 4) collar added, 5)1-cord added to edges. Some structural elements are hidden (grafted seams). Some of what appear to be structural elements aren't (phony seams). Other structural elements have become style elements (short rows in contrasting color).

Mosaic pat (2-st rep)

Rows 1 and 2 With MC, knit. Row 3 (RS) With CC, *k1, sl 1 with yarn in back; rep from*. Row 4 *Sl 1 with yarn in front, k1; rep from*. Rows 5 and 6 With MC, knit. Rows 7 and 8 With CC, knit.

Body

With larger needles and MC, cast on 120 (152, 180) sts. Row 1 (RS) K30 (38, 45) (right front), sl 1 with yarn in back (side seam), k58 (74, 88) (back), sl 1 with yarn in back (side seam), k30 (38, 45) (left front). Row 2 (WS) K30 (38, 45), p 1, k58 (74, 88), p1, k30 (38, 45). Rep last 2 rows until there are 58 (59, 60) ridges in MC. With CC, k 4 rows.

Shape sleeves and back yoke

Next row (RS) Cont phony seam, k90 (114, 135), *then k rem 30 (38, 45) sts with scrap yarn. Sl last 30 sts back to left-hand needle and k them again with CC, casting on 15 (20, 25) sts at end of row—135 (172, 205) sts. Next row K to last 30 sts and rep from* of previous row—150 (192, 230) sts. With MC, k across all sts. Work mosaic spat between phony seams and beg sleeve shaping as foll: Every CC ridge is worked from cuff to cuff while every MC ridge is a short row. The first short ridge extends 2 sts beyond the phony seam. Each succeeding MC ridge is 2 sts longer than the previous one. Work until 7 (8, 9) pattern stripes have been completed minus the final CC row.

Shape neck and front yoke

In final CC row, work the center 22 (26, 32) sts with scrap yarn, then sl 11 (13, 16) sts back to the left needle and knit them with CC. On half the sts, work one front section, reversing short row lengths, end with 2 CC ridges. Do not bind off. Place the sts on a spare needle or length of scrap yarn. Work the other front to correspond.

Finishing

Remove scrap yarn from sleeve/yoke shaping and place 30 (38, 45) sts each side on hold. Fold sides of bottom half (up to scrap yarn) inward to form fronts. Fold top of sleeve/yoke section down to neck scrap yarn to form sleeves and front yoke. Weave underarm and front seams.

Sizes 4 (6, 8). Shown in size 4.

Measurements Chest (buttoned) 24 (30, 36)". Length 18 (19, 20)".

Yarn 8 (10, 12) balls worsted weight yarn (each 1¾oz/50g, approx 110yd/100m) in Yellow (MC). 3 (4, 4) balls in Navy (CC).

Needles Size 8 (5mm) needles, *or size to obtain gauge.* Size 6 (4mm) double-pointed needles (dpn).

Extras Stitch holders and markers. Six ⅞" buttons.

Gauge 20 sts and 40 rows to 4" (10cm) in garter st using size 8 (5mm) needles.

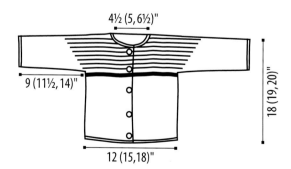

4½ (5, 6½)"

9 (11½, 14)"

12 (15,18)"

18 (19, 20)"

Neckband

Remove scrap yarn from neck. With CC, k 6 rows. Place sts on hold.

I-cord edging

Place markers for 6 buttonholes (on left front for boys, on right front for girls), the first just below collar, and 5 others spaced approx 3" apart. Beg at lower edge at phony seam and with dpn, cast on 3 sts. Work attached I-cord around lower edges, along fronts and around collar edges, working 2 rows of unattached I-cord at each buttonhole marker. Weave I-cord ends tog. Sew buttons on.

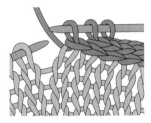

Elizabeth Zimmermann's Attached 3-st I-cord edging with contrasting color

Note. Pick up sts for I-cord edgings at a ratio of 2 sts for every 3 cast-on or bound-off sts and 3 sts for every 4 rows. For ease in handling, pick up 15-20 sts at a time.

1. With RS facing, contrasting color and dpn, pick up sts along edge.

2. With 2nd dpn, cast on 3 sts, *return sts to LH needle, k2, sl 1, yo, k picked-up st, p2sso; rep from* around.

3. Sew last 3 sts to cast-on sts.

Hickory, dickory, dock...

Hickory, dickory, dock,

The mouse ran up the clock.

The clock struck one,

The mouse ran down!

Hickory, dickory, dock.

Toys

Critter Clothes

EXPERIENCED

When my daughter Amaran was in the
fourth grade, I made this sweater for
her and her friend Xena's Molly dolls.
I wanted a design that was both colorful
enough to keep the knitting interesting
and easy enough to finish quickly.
The color choices came from Amaran.
She has always loved color,
and at that time,
green was her favorite.

Back

With smaller needles and MC, cast on 41 sts. Change to larger needles. **Row 1** (RS) *K1 MC, p1 A; rep from* to last st, k1 MC. **Row 2** P1 MC, *k1 C, p1 MC; rep from* to end. **Row 3** *K1 MC, p1 E; rep from* to last st, k1 MC. **Row 4** P1 MC; *k1 G, p1 MC; rep from* to end. **Beg Chart A: Row 1** (RS) Work 41 sts Chart A. Work through row 36 of Chart A. **Row 37** K 7, slip next 15 sts onto holder, join MC, k to end. Cont to end of Chart A, work decs as indicated.

Left Front

With smaller needles and MC, cast on 20 sts. Change to larger needles. **Row 1** (RS) *P1 A, k1 MC; rep from * to end. **Row 2** *P1 MC, k1 C; rep from* to end. **Row 3** *P1 E, k1 MC; rep from* to end. **Row 4** *P1 MC, k1 G; rep from* to end. **Beg Chart A: Row 1** (RS) Work sts 1 to 20 of Chart A. Cont Chart A to end, shaping neck as indicated and using MC only from row 28 to end.

Right Front

With smaller needles and MC, cast on 20 sts. Change to larger needles. **Row 1** (RS) *K1 MC, p1 A; rep from* to end. **Row 2** *K1 C, p1 MC; rep from* to end. **Row 3** *K1 MC, p1 E; rep from* to end. **Row 4** *K1 G, p1 MC; rep from* to end. **Beg Chart A: Row 1** (RS) Work sts 22 to 41 of Chart A. Cont Chart A to end, shaping neck as indicated and using MC only from row 28 to end.

Sleeves

With smaller needles and MC, cast on 27 sts. Change to larger needles. **Row 1** (RS) K1 MC, *p1 A, k1 MC; rep from* to end. **Row 2** *P1 MC, k1 C; rep from* to last st, p1 MC. **Row 3** K1 MC, *p1 E, k1 MC; rep from* to end. **Row 4** *P1 MC, k1 G; rep from* to last st, p1 MC. **Beg Chart B: Row 1** (RS) Work 27 sts of Chart B. Cont Chart B to end of row 28, shaping as indicated.

Finishing

Block pieces. Sew shoulders.

Neckband

With RS facing, smaller needles and MC, beg at right front neck edge and pick up and k11 sts to shoulder, 2 sts down back neck, k across 15 sts from holder, 2 sts to holder, 11 sts to left front neck—41 sts. **Row 1** (WS) P1 MC, *k1 F, p1 MC; rep from* to end. **Row 2** (RS) K1 MC, *p1 D, k1 MC; rep from* to end. **Row 3** P1 MC, *k1 A, p1 MC; rep from* to end. With MC, bind off in rib .

Buttonband

With RS facing, smaller needles and MC, beg at top of left front neckband and pick up and k32 sts to lower edge. **Row 1** (WS) P1 MC, *k1 G, p1 MC; rep from* to end. **Row 2** (RS) *K1 MC, p1

Size For an 18" doll.

Measurements Chest 14". Length approx 6¼".

Yarn 1 ball sport weight yarn (each 1¾oz/50g, approx 136yd/124m) in Green (MC). Small amounts of Bright red (A), Red (B), Pink (C), Orange (D), Light orange (E), Gold (F) and Yellow (G).

Needles One pair each sizes 2 and 3 (3 and 3.25mm) needles, *or size to obtain gauge.*

Extras Stitch holders. Five ½" buttons.

Gauge 25 sts and 27 rows to 4" (10cm) over Chart pat using size 3 (3.25mm) needles.

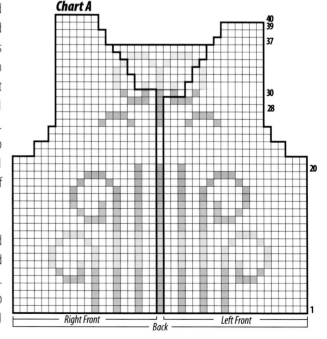

Chart A

Right Front | Back | Left Front

E; rep from* to last 2 sts, with MC, k1, p1. **Row 3** With MC, k1, p1, *k1 D, p1 MC; rep from* to end. **Row 4** *K1 MC, p1 C; rep from* to last 2 sts, with MC, k1, p1. **Row 5** With MC, k1, p1, *k1 A, p1 MC; rep from* to end. With MC, work 1 more row in rib. With MC, bind off in rib.

Buttonhole band

Work to match buttonband, making buttonholes in Row 3 as foll: work 4 sts, bind off 1 st, [work until 5 sts on right needle, bind off 1 st] 4 times; work last 2 sts. On row 4, cast on 1 st over bound-off st from previous row.

Set in sleeves. Sew side and sleeve seams. Sew buttons on.

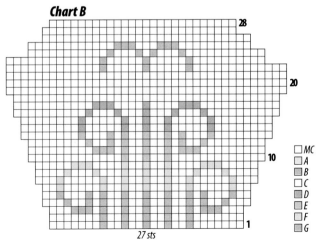

Chart B

27 sts

- ☐ MC
- ☐ A
- ▨ B
- ☐ C
- ▨ D
- ☐ E
- ☐ F
- ▨ G

EXPERIENCED

The adventure started when my friend's
5-year-old, Natalie, began her fall
campaign to beg her parents for a pony
for Christmas. As there was no way
this wish could be granted,
I decided to make a pony for her!
My best advice for knitting toys
for children is: make it very tiny
or go really big...

Body, head and legs

Knit all the pieces foll the charts. The notes by each chart indicate the number of pieces to make . Work all incs and decs after the first st and before the last st for full-fashioned shaping.

Finishing

Block pieces. If lining is desired, cut muslin pieces to match knit pieces. Using diagrams and photo as guide, sew the knit pieces together, stuffing each lightly as you go. If constructing a muslin lining as well, construct the pony around the muslin, stuffing it as you go. Make fringe out of the black yarn for the mane and tail.

With black yarn and outline st (p. 70), work centers of the eyes. With cream, buttonhole stitch around the centers (see detail photo).

Blanket stitch

Work the same as button-hole stitch, but space the stitches apart.

Finished measurements Height 30". Length from ear to tail 30".

Yarn 18 balls worsted weight yarn (each 1¾ oz/50g, approx 110yd/100m) in Brown tweed. 8 balls in Black and 4 balls in White.

Needles Size 7 (4.5mm) needles, *or size to obtain gauge.*

Extras Four 8 oz. bags of stuffing.

Gauge 18 sts and 28 rows to 4" (10cm) over St st using size 7 (4.5mm) needles.

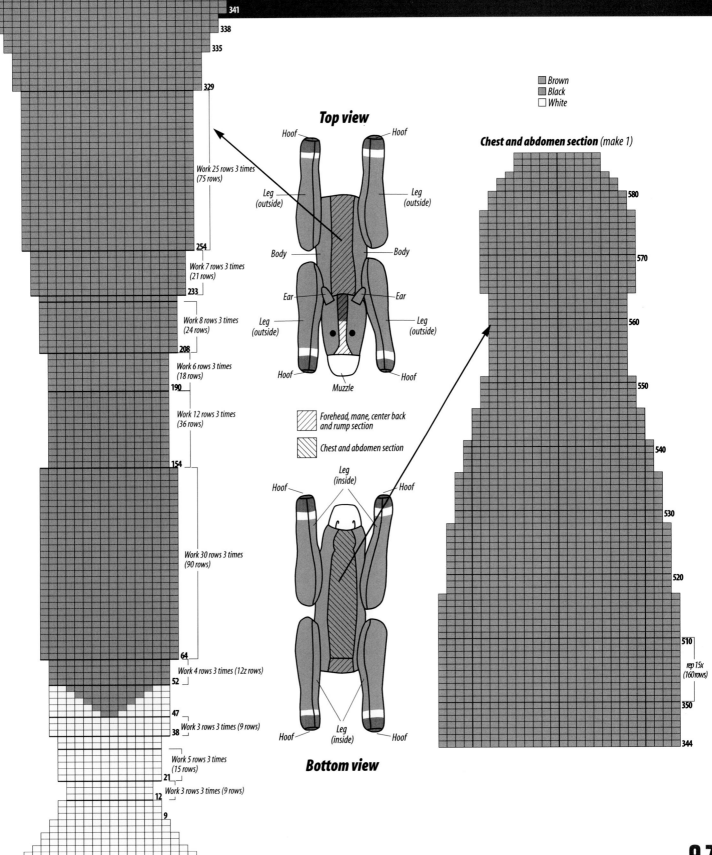

341
338
335
329

Work 25 rows 3 times
(75 rows)

254

Work 7 rows 3 times
(21 rows)

233

Work 8 rows 3 times
(24 rows)

208

Work 6 rows 3 times
(18 rows)

190

Work 12 rows 3 times
(36 rows)

154

Work 30 rows 3 times
(90 rows)

64

Work 4 rows 3 times (12z rows)

52

47

Work 3 rows 3 times (9 rows)

38

Work 5 rows 3 times
(15 rows)

21

Work 3 rows 3 times (9 rows)

12

9

1

22 sts

Top view

Hoof   Hoof

Leg
(outside)   Leg
(outside)

Body   Body

Ear   Ear

Leg
(outside)   Leg
(outside)

Hoof   Hoof

Muzzle

☐ Brown
☐ Black
☐ White

⬚ Forehead, mane, center back
and rump section

⬚ Chest and abdomen section

Leg
(inside)

Hoof   Hoof

Leg
(inside)

Hoof   Hoof

Bottom view

Chest and abdomen section *(make 1)*

580
570
560
550
540
530
520
510

rep 15x
(160 rows)

350
344

97

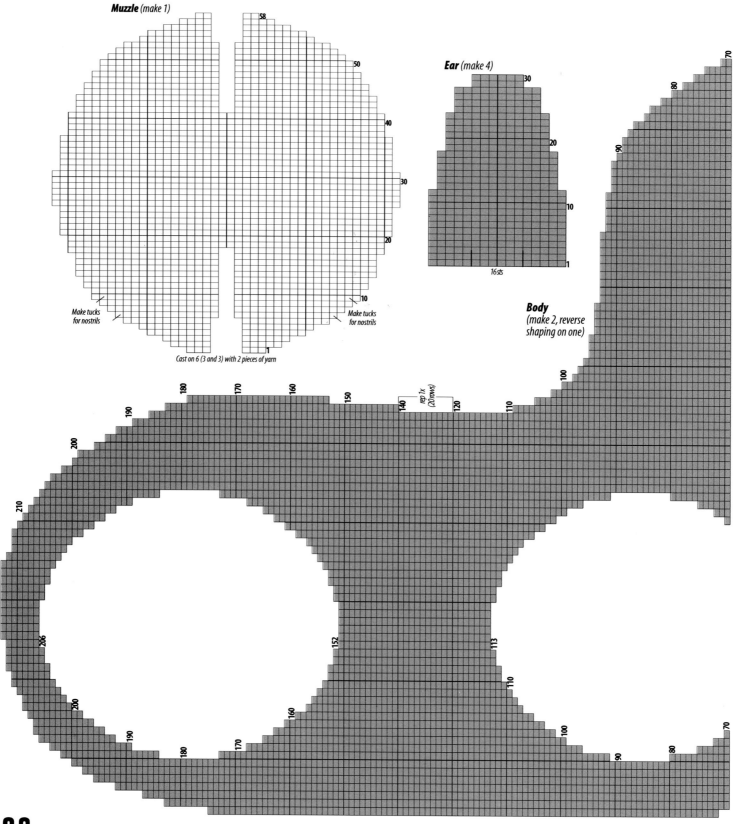

Muzzle (make 1)

58

50

40

30

20

10

1

Make tucks
for nostrils

Make tucks
for nostrils

Cast on 6 (3 and 3) with 2 pieces of yarn

Ear (make 4)

30

20

10

1

16 sts

Body
(make 2, reverse
shaping on one)

70

80

90

100

rep 1x
(20 rows)

110

113

110

100

90

80

70

140

120

150

160

152

160

170

180

170

180

190

190

200

200

206

210

98

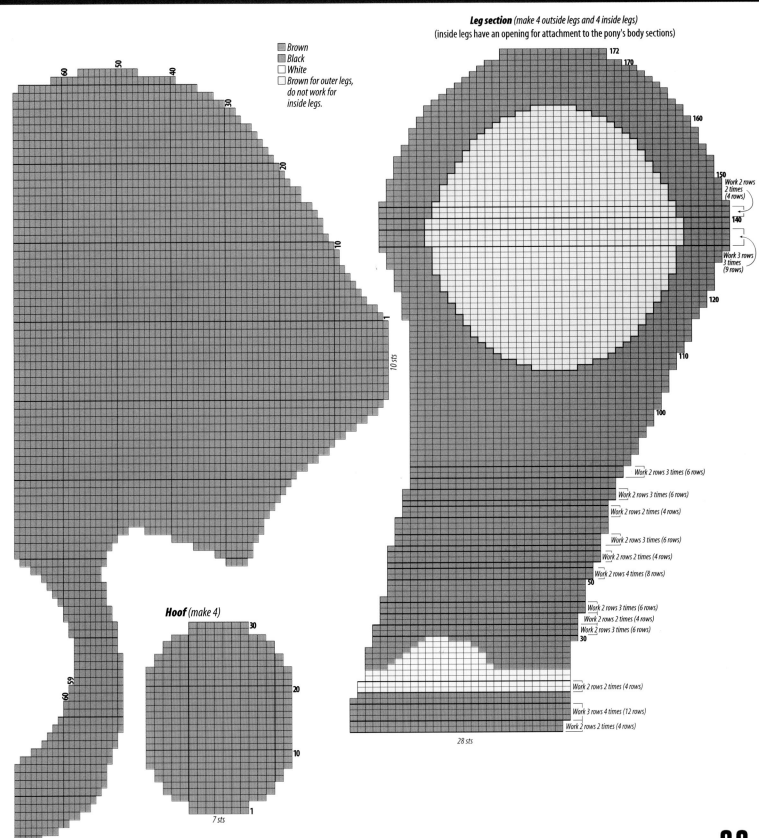

Brown
Black
White
Brown for outer legs,
do not work for
inside legs.

Leg section (make 4 outside legs and 4 inside legs)
(inside legs have an opening for attachment to the pony's body sections)

172
170

160

150
Work 2 rows
2 times
(4 rows)

140

Work 3 rows
3 times
(9 rows)

120

110

100

Work 2 rows 3 times (6 rows)

Work 2 rows 3 times (6 rows)

Work 2 rows 2 times (4 rows)

Work 2 rows 3 times (6 rows)

Work 2 rows 2 times (4 rows)

Work 2 rows 4 times (8 rows)

50

Work 2 rows 3 times (6 rows)

Work 2 rows 2 times (4 rows)

Work 2 rows 3 times (6 rows)

30

Work 2 rows 2 times (4 rows)

Work 3 rows 4 times (12 rows)

Work 2 rows 2 times (4 rows)

28 sts

60
50
40

30

20

10

1

10 sts

Hoof (make 4)

30

20

10

1

7 sts

60
59

9 9

Bird of Paradise

MARY LEE HERRICK
NORFOLK, VIRGINIA

EXPERIENCED

This bird's feet are pipe cleaners bent so that it will stand on the edge of a shelf or on top of a computer monitor.

Measurement Body approx 6" tall.

Yarn 1 ball sport weight yarn (each 1¾oz/50g, approx 136yd/124m) in Multi-colored novelty yarn (MC). Small amounts of solid Yellow (CC1), Orange (CC2), Bright blue (CC3) and Black (CC4).

Needles Set of double-pointed needles (dpn) in size 5 (3.75mm), *or size to obtain gauge.*

Extras Stuffing. One pair 12mm black safety lock eyes. Two brown pipe-cleaners. Stitch markers.

Gauge 22 sts and 26 rows to 4" (10cm) over St st using size 5 (3.75mm) needles and MC.

Body

With dpn and MC, cast on 6 sts and divide evenly over 3 dpn. Place marker and join, being careful not to twist sts. **Rnd 1 [K1, M1] 6 times—12 sts, 4 sts each dpn. **Rnds 2, 4, 6 and 8** Knit. **Rnd 3** [K1, M1, k2, M1] 4 times—20 sts. **Rnd 5** [K1, M1] 20 times—40 sts. **Rnd 7** [K2, M1] 20 times—60 sts. Work back and forth in rows as foll: **Rearrange sts: Row 1** (RS) With MC, k21 to first dpn; with CC1, k18 to 2nd dpn; with MC, k21 to 3rd dpn, turn. **Row 2** (WS) P in colors and sts as established. Rep last 2 rows 3 times more.

Shape back

Cont in colors as established, bind off 2 sts at beg of next 4 rows—52 sts. Dec 1 st beg of next 6 rows—46 sts.

Shape neck

Join rnd With MC, k around. **Next rnd** K1, [k2tog, k3, k2tog, k2] 5 times—36 sts. K 1 rnd.

Head

Next rnd [K3, M1] 12 times—48 sts. K 16 rnds. **Shape Head: Rnd 1** [K2, k2tog] 12 times—36 sts. **Rnds 2, 4 and 6** Knit. **Rnd 3** [K1, k2tog] 12 times—24 sts. **Rnd 5** [K2tog] 6 times—6 sts. Cut yarn, leaving a 12" tail. Pull tail through all sts and leaving opening loose, complete stuffing. Pull sts tog tightly and fasten off.

Wings (make 2)

With dpn and MC, cast on 27 sts. Do not join. Beg with a p row, work 10 rows in St st. Work 13 rows more and dec 1 st each side every row. Cut yarn, pull through last st and secure. Fold wing in half and with any CC, sew side seam. Beg 2 rows below neck shaping and sew wings to body, just beside CC1.

Beak

With dpn and CC2, cast on 28 sts and divide over 3 dpn as foll: 7 sts each to first and 3rd dpn, 14 sts to 2nd dpn. Place marker and join, being careful not to twist sts. K 6 rnds.

Shape beak

K20, wrap yarn around next st and turn (WT). P13, WT. K14, k2tog, k10, ssk (end of needle 1)—26 sts. K13, WT, p12, WT, k11, ssk, k2tog, k8, ssk—23 sts. K2tog, k10, WT, p10, WT, k9, ssk, k2tog, k6, ssk—19 sts. K2tog, k17—18 sts. **Next rnd** With CC3, k2tog, k6, ssk, k2tog, k4, ssk—14 sts. **Next rnd** With CC4, k14. K2tog, k4, ssk, k2tog, k2, ssk—10 sts. [K2tog] 5 times—5 sts. Cut yarn, leaving a 12" tail. Pull yarn tail through 5 sts once, then through first st of rnd once more. Pull tail tog tightly and fasten off. Stuff nose. Sew in place between neck and eyes.

Finishing

Lightly stuff head. Stuff beak and sew in place. Attach eyes above beak. Finish stuffing head and body, sew back seams. Sew running st around neck, tie ends of yarn tightly to define neck, tuck ends inside bird with crochet hook.

EDITOR'S NOTE **Head feathers** Cut 5 strands of MC, each approx 2" long. Fold in half and attach.

Tail feathers Cut 6 strands MC, each approx 5½" long. Fold 1½" in from one end and attach.

Feet Cut a 4" piece of pipe cleaner and sl it through lower MC section, folding it in half. Cut one 1¾" piece and one 1¼" piece of 2nd pipe cleaner and attach as claws. Rep for 2nd foot.

EXPERIENCED

Tail

With dpn and MC, cast on 3 sts and work 2" in I-Cord. Inc 1 st in next row and work 4-st I-cord for 1½". **Next rnd** Knit and divide over 3 dpn: K1, M1, k3; place marker for beg of rnd—5 sts. K for 2" more. **Next rnd** K1, M1, k4—6 sts. K for 1". **Next rnd** K2, M1, k4— 7 sts. K for 1". **Next rnd** K3, M1, k4—8 sts. K for 1". **Next rnd** K4, M1, k4—9 sts. **Next rnd** K5, M1, k4—10 sts.

Body

Reading each chart rnd from right to left only, work as foll: **Beg Chart: Rnd 1** K1 CC, k2 MC, pm, k2 MC, k1 CC, k2 MC, pm, k2 MC—10 sts. **Rnd 2** K2 MC, k1 CC, M1 MC, sl marker, M1 MC, k2 MC, k1 CC, k2 MC, M1 MC, sl marker, M1 MC, k1 CC, k1 MC—14 sts. Work chart as established through Rnd 22—42 sts. Then work rnds 13-32 twice more, then rnds 13-17 once. Body meas approx 8". Cut CC.

Neck

Next rnd With MC, [k2tog, k19] twice—40 sts. **Next rnd** Knit. **Rearrange sts as foll** 10 sts each to first and 3rd dpn, 20 sts to 2nd dpn. Stuff body to neck. **Shape head: Rnd 1** On first dpn, k to last 3 sts, k2tog, k1; on 2nd dpn, k1, ssk, k to last 3 sts, k2tog, k1; on 3rd dpn, k1, ssk, k to end—36 sts. **Rnd 2** Knit. Rep last 2 rnds 5 times more—16 sts. Stuff head, attach safety eyes (into 3rd st from each end of 2nd dpn, approx 5 rows down) Cont to dec as established twice more—8 sts (2 sts each on first and 3rd dpn, 4 sts on 2nd dpn). Stuff rem part of head. Cut yarn, leaving a 4" tail. Draw tail through rem sts, tighten and fasten off. With 1 strand of MC and tapestry needle, work basting st around entire neck in last rnd 15 of chart. Tighten gently, secure.

Feet (make 4)

With dpn and MC, cast on 15 sts and divide evenly over 3 dpn. Pm and join, being careful not to twist sts. K every rnd until piece measures 2" from beg. **Shape toes: Rnd 1** [K1, k2tog] 5 times—10 sts. K 3 rnds. **Next rnd** [K2tog] 5 times—5 sts. Cut yarn, leaving a 7" tail. Draw tail through rem sts, pull tog tightly. Do not cut yarn. Stuff foot. With rem tail of yarn, work basting st around entire foot, just below beg of toe shaping. Tighten gently, fasten off. With strand of MC and tapestry needle, work basting st around entire leg, 1 row in from cast on edge. Tighten gently and fasten off. Attach to body.

Finishing

Using photo as guide, use CC to embroider toes. Make knot at tail end. Tie ribbon around neck.

I have to thank my mother for my love of yarn and knitting (and for patiently teaching me!). I remember seeing her knit with four needles and wondering how she could manage it. Once I knitted my first pair of socks, I understood. Basically this pattern is one large sock (with tail) and four little socks for feet. It's really quick and easy once you master the double-pointed needles.

Measurement Approx 10 ½" long (not including tail).

Yarn 1 ball sport weight yarn (each 1¾oz/50g, approx 136yd/124m) in White (MC) and in Variegated (CC).

Needles Set of 4 double-pointed needles (dpn) in size 6 (4mm), *or size to obtain gauge.*

Extras Stuffing. One pair 12mm safety lock eyes. Approx 22" length of ¼" ribbon. Stitch markers.

Gauge 24 sts and 22 rows to 4" (10cm) over Chart pat using size 6 (4mm) needles.

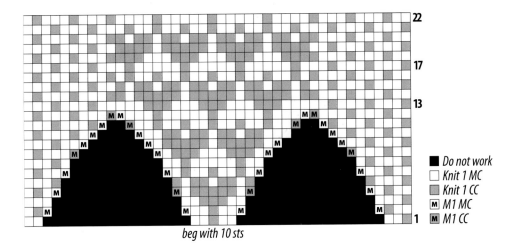

22

17

13

1

- ■ Do not work
- □ Knit 1 MC
- ▨ Knit 1 CC
- Ⓜ M1 MC
- Ⓜ M1 CC

beg with 10 sts

EXPERIENCED

I raise angora goats from which mohair comes. I shear them myself, holding them in my lap and kissing their noses if they find shearing a frightening experience.
Then, I wash the hair. After it has dried on big screens in the wind and sun, I pick it apart by hand, card it, and it's ready for dyeing or spinning, or both.
This MoBear's hair is Clover's first clipping. MoBear's insides are stuffed with one of the older goat's hair. MoBear's heels are turned like all my socks, and her profile is all her own.
Her eyes are antique jet buttons. I was going to have articulating hips and shoulders but it didn't work.

Measurement Approx 14" tall.

Yarns Bear approx 2 oz of worsted weight mohair.

Sweater Approx 2 oz of worsted weight mohair; small amounts of 3 contrast colors for logo and nose.

Needles Set of double-pointed needles (dpn) in size 7 (3.75mm) (for bear) and size 9 (4.5mm) (for sweater), *or size to obtain gauge.*

Extras Size C/2 (3mm) crochet hook. Stuffing. Two round buttons for eyes or one pair 12mm safety lock eyes. Stitch markers.

Gauge 18 sts and 24 rows to 4" (10cm) over St st using size 7 (3.75mm) needles.

BEAR

Legs (make 2)

With larger dpn cast on 6 sts, leaving a tail, and divide evenly over 3 dpn. Place marker (pm) and join, being careful not to twist sts. **Rnd 1 [K1, M1] 6 times—12 sts (4 sts each dpn). **Rnd 2** Knit. **Rnd 3** *[K1, M1] twice, k1; rep from* around—20 sts. K every rnd until piece measures 4" from beg.**

Divide for heel Next rnd K3 and sl these 3 sts and last 3 sts of rnd onto first dpn; leave rem 14 sts on hold. Work on these 6 sts only. **Row 1** (WS) Sl 1, p5. **Row 2** Sl 1, k5. **Rows 3-6** Rep rows 1-2. Do not turn.

Gusset With empty dpn, pick up and k 5 sts along side of heel; with 2nd dpn, k across 14 sts; with 3rd dpn, pick up and k 5 sts along other side of heel, then k3 heel sts; sl rem 3 heel sts onto first dpn (beg of rnd is at center heel)—30 sts. **Next rnd** On first dpn, k to last 3 sts, ssk, k1; k across 2nd dpn; on 3rd dpn, k1, k2tog, k to end—28 sts. **Next rnd** Knit. Rep last 2 rnds until 20 sts rem. K 5 rnds. **Next rnd** [K2tog] twice, k to last 4 sts, [k2tog] twice—16 sts. K 1 rnd. **Next rnd** [K2tog, k4, k2tog] twice—12 sts. K 1 rnd. Weave tail through cast-on sts at beg of leg, tighten and fasten off. Stuff leg firmly. **Next rnd** [K2tog, k2, k2tog] twice—8 sts. Complete stuffing. Cut yarn, leaving a 12" tail. Graft front 4 sts tog with 4 sts from back.

Arms (make 2)

Work as for Leg from** to **. **Next rnd** K2, k2tog, k12, k2tog, k2—18 sts. K 1 rnd. **Next rnd** K1, k2tog, k2, k2tog, k4, k2tog, k2, k2tog, k1—14 sts. K 1 rnd. **Next rnd** [K1, k2tog] twice; k2, [k2tog, k1] twice—10 sts. K 1 rnd. Weave tail through cast-on sts at beg of arm, tighten and fasten off. Stuff arm firmly. Cut yarn, leaving a 12" tail. Graft front 5 sts tog with rem 5 sts.

Body

With dpn cast on 6 sts, leaving a tail, and divide evenly over 3 dpn. Pm and join, being careful not to twist sts. **Rnd 1 [K1, M1] 6 times—12 sts (4 sts each dpn). **Rnds 2 and 4** Knit. **Rnd 3** [K1, M1, k3, M1] 3 times—18 sts. **Rnd 5** [K1, M1, k5, M1] 3 times—24 sts.** In same way, cont to inc every other rnd until there are 14 sts on each dpn—42 sts. K 5 rnds. **Next rnd** K1, k2tog, k to last 2 sts, ssk—40 sts. **Next rnd** Knit. Rep last 2 rnds until 20 sts rem. K 10 rows. Cut yarn, leaving a 12" tail. Weave beg tail through cast-on sts at beg of body, tighten and fasten off. Pull 2nd tail through all sts and leaving opening loose, stuff body firmly. Pull sts tog tightly, secure and fasten off.

Head

Work as for Body from** to **. Cont to inc every other rnd until there are 12 sts on each dpn—36 sts. K 7 rnds. **Shape forehead: Next rnd** K15, M1, k6, M1, k15—38 sts. Pm for eye position at M1's. **Next rnd** K15, M1, k8, M1, k15—40 sts. Cont to inc 2 sts every rnd 6 times more—52 sts. Pm for center of ears at M1's of last rnd.

Shape back of head

Rnd 1 K2, [k3, k2tog] 10 times—42 sts. **Rnds 2, 4, 6, 8, 10 and 12** Knit. **Rnd 3** K2, [k2, k2tog] 10 times—32 sts. **Rnd 5** [K2, k2tog] 8 times—24 sts. **Rnd 7** [K1, k2tog] 8 times—16 sts. **Rnd 9** [K2, k2tog] 4 times—12 sts. *Note* Attach safety lock eyes now. Stuff head firmly. **Rnd 11** [K2tog] 6 times—6 sts. Cut yarn, leaving a 12" tail. Pull tail through all sts and leaving opening loose, complete stuffing. Pull sts tightly, secure and fasten off.

Finishing

Ears With dpn, pick up and k 6 sts, using marker to center ear. Beg with a k row, work 4 rows in St st. **Next row** (RS) Ssk, k2, k2tog—4 sts. **Next row** [P2tog] twice—2 sts. Bind off. **2nd half of ear** With dpn, pick up and k 6 sts behind sts just worked. Work to match first half. Place small amount of stuffing in center of ear. With crochet hook, work 1 row dc through both thicknesses to close ear. *Note* Working fewer sts around the ear will tilt the ear forward. If safety lock eyes have not been used, sew buttons in place. Using photo as guide, embroider nose using satin st, covering up cast-on row of head. Sew legs and arms to body.

SWEATER

With smaller dpn, cast on 50 sts and divide over 3 dpn as foll: 17 sts each on first and last dpn, 16 sts on 2nd dpn). Pm and join, being careful not to twist sts. Work 3 rnds in k1, p1 rib. Change to larger dpn and k 20 rnds. **Divide for back and front: Next rnd** K15 (back), bind off next 10 sts, k until there are 15 sts on dpn and leave these 15 sts on hold for front, bind off 10 sts. **Back** Work 12 rows in St st over 15 sts for Back. Bind off 3 sts at beg of next 2 rows. Leave rem 9 sts on hold for back neck. **Front** Join yarn and work 6 rows in St st. **Shape neck: Next row** K6, join a 2nd ball of yarn and bind off 3 sts, work to end. Working both sides at same time, dec 1 st at each neck edge every row 3 times—3 sts each side. Work 2 rows even. Bind off all sts.

Finishing

Block pieces lightly. Sew shoulder seams.

Sleeves

With RS facing and larger dpn, pick up and k 24 sts around armhole. K 17 rnds. Change to smaller dpn and work 3 rnds in k1, p1 rib. Bind off loosely in rib. Rep for 2nd sleeve.

Neckband With smaller dpn, k 9 sts from back neck, then pick up and k 15 sts around neck—24 sts. Work 3 rnds in k1, p1 rib. Bind off loosely in rib.

Using photo as guide, use contrast color to embroider logo (or initials of choice) to front of sweater.

**Downstairs, Stitches West '98
is in full swing: the market and the
classrooms are abuzz, while in the
Knitting Corner young girls and boys
pick up needles for the first time.
Upstairs, the Presidential Suite
of the Oakland Marriott
resembles a child's fantasy world;
Knitter's Magazine's kids contest
sweaters and toys are everywhere.
Here among all the colorful entries,
our judges feel, well—
like kids themselves . . . .**

Kids, Kids, Kids began in 1997 with a call for entries for the *Knitter's Magazine* contest, "Knitting is for Kids, Too." "Kids bring out the best in us," we said to our readers. "They refresh us and remind us to take time to stop and play. And knitting for kids can be the best—the colors are joyous, the knitting time is manageable, and the audience is enthusiastic."

The next few months things must have been happening, but we weren't there to see. When the entries arrived in January 1998, what a surprise! We were amazed as we opened the boxes and envelopes, first in Sioux Falls and again, later when our judges gathered at Stitches in California. The range, variety, and number of exceptional pieces were exciting. Now the challenge was ours.

And the winners are "We gasped when we saw 'The Pony' (p. 96), 'Hansel and Gretel' (p. 68), 'Hiawatha' (p. 44)...." says judge Sally Melville, author of *Sally Melville's Styles* (who has a son and daughter in college). "This isn't just knitting for kids—it's heirlooms, to be treasured for years to come!"

Sally's enthusiasm is shared by our other judges: Media Consultant Candi Jensen (who recently became a grandmother) and Classic Elite Creative Director Kristin Nicholas (who has a baby girl). "It was difficult to judge this contest," Sally says. "We were faced with such a huge range of shapes and sizes, knitting ability, technique, yarns—and creativity. When people think of knitting for kids or babies there's so much out there that says you need to use the obligatory blue, yellow and pink. We got almost none of that. Everything is bright, wonderful, colorful. It shows a change in what people think of as kids' knits."

Judges Sally, Candi and Kristin with a
few of their favorites.

Selecting the winners was the next challenge. (Check the names marked with an asterisk on p. 106 to see if you agree with the judges.) Then the cover sweater (Cindy Brook's 'Beribboned!,' p. 56) was awarded the People's Choice Award by Stitches participants.

"I loved reading the accompanying letters as much as I loved the entries," says Kristin Nicholas. "Irene Sinclair who made 'Emily's Sweater' (p. 32) talks about the 40 packs of Kool-Aid and the process, but also about getting her grand-daughter involved. The sweater is great—but the best part is involving a kid." We were sure you also would enjoy meeting the knitters in this way, so each pattern begins with their reflections.

The kid test Since these knits were inspired by and knit for real kids, it was essential to put kids with the knits in this book. We did choose to show the infant garments close up and flat, for ours, yours and several babies' sake. A few other sweaters weren't around when the kids were or needed a closer-up view. But most were photographed on kids by Alexis Xenakis and our *Knitter's* team including Fashion Editor Nancy J. Thomas: in the park in Chicago, on the beach in Miami, at the zoo in San Diego and around the neighborhood in Sioux Falls, South Dakota. The kids were great, but best of all they liked the knits! (Our special thanks go to Travis Dunham, Tyler Wilson and his cousin Danielle Fantroy, and the Hoffman family for being available when the sun came out, and to the friendly people and animals of the San Diego Zoo.)

Into your hands This book is the second in our series of contest books, and Graphic Designer Bob Natz customized the design to reflect the first, *Socks, Socks, Socks,* and fit the images and mood of a kid's book .

Bob explains, "Headlines are Myriad Black, upper and lower case. Contestants and knitting skill level information is Bold Helvetica, caps. These elements provide a soft contrast to the text, which is Myriad light, condensed. The intent was to provide the maximum readability while accommodating various text lengths. Subheads are bold for accent and reference, and intros are Folio Medium."

Kids, Kids, Kids was produced using Macintosh Power PCs; Quark Xpress; Adobe Illustrator and Photoshop; and an Epson Rip Station 5000 ink-jet printer under the watchful eye of Publishing Services Director David Xenakis and our dedicated staff: Book Production Manager Lynda Selle, Digital Color Specialist Daren Morgan, Production Chief Carol Skallerud, and Production Artists Kellie Meissner and Jay Reeve.

Kids, Kids, Kids is not just for kids; it's for the eternally-young knitter in all of us.

— *Elaine Rowley, Sioux Falls, SD*

A wonderful collection and a tough job for our judges: Sally Melville and Susannah Heath's nearly-life-sized pony …

Colophon

… Kristin Nicholas and Rita Garrity-Knudson's 'Hansel and Gretel' with the witch and her gingerbread house …

… Candi Jensen and Kerry Fletcher-Garbisch's 'Hiawatha' …

An Index of the Knitters

This alphabetical listing of the knitters gives a detail of the knitted item, its name, the suggested skill level, and, in bold, the page on which it is found.

*Prize winners in the Kids contest.

We can't publish all the knitting books in the world—only the finest.

We are knitting enthusiasts and book lovers. Our mission is simple: to produce quality books that showcase the beauty of the knitting and give our readers inspiration, confidence, and skill-building instructions.

Publishing begins as a partnership between author and publisher. XRX Books attracts the best authors and designers in the knitting universe because we share their passion for excellence. But books also require a shared vision: photographer Alexis Xenakis and his team bring the garments and fabrics to glorious life. This is where our journey begins.

XRX wants to know

Cutting-edge computer technology allows us to focus on editing and designing our publications. XRX Books Editor Elaine Rowley can exchange files from South Dakota with our knitting editor in New York or our authors, wherever they happen to live, within a matter of minutes. Our digital consultant, David Xenakis, and his team insure accuracy of color and texture in our images. Graphic Artist Bob Natz, believing that design is not good unless it functions well, produces beautiful, easy-to-read pages.

Now those pages are in your hands and your journey begins.

Tell us what you think:

- **by mail**
  XRX Books
  PO Box 1525
  Sioux Falls, South Dakota
  57101-1525

- **by phone**
  605-338-2450

- **by fax**
  605-338-2994

- **by e-mail**
  erowley@xrx-inc.com

- **on xrx-inc.com**
  You may visit our XRX Books site
  on the World Wide Web: www.xrx-inc.com

- **On our Knitter's OnLine forums:**
  Join the conversation and post your reactions and comments in our book discussion bulletin boards:
  www.knittinguniverse.com/script/webx.dll?knitalk

We look forward to hearing from you. New journeys are under way.

Other Publications

Sally Melville Styles

Magnificent Mittens

Ethnic Socks and Stockings

The Great American Afghan

Knitter's Magazine

Weaver's Magazine

Socks•Socks•Socks

The Best of Knitters

 BOOKS